Pranayama

and

Breathwork

Workbook

A journey with breath

Everyday tools for a better life

Experience the difference

James Beard

Sacred Systems
PO Box 23962
San Diego, CA 92193

Cover and interior design James Beard

ISBN-13: 978-1542860529

ISBN-10: 1542860520

Printed in the United States of America by Createspace

The intention of this writing is to share pranayama and Breathwork exercises I found helpful in my life. It is not my intention to replace medical care or give medical or psychological advice. I, the author and publisher and distributors, will not and cannot be held accountable for prosecution for any loss or harm, be it physical, mental or emotional, do to the material and intentions within this book.

In the following stories, some of the names have been changed as a courtesy. What was, was. All is forgiven and the lessons learned are much appreciated.

Peace

Gratitude

First of all I am grateful to the spirit of breath. It has entertained and comforted me throughout my life. It has fascinated, healed and empowered me in the most extraordinary way. Discovering your breath can do the same for you.

I am grateful to the International Breathwork Foundation (IBF) for holding a yearly Global Inspirational Conference (GIC) since 1993.

My thanks goes out to Seymour Goblin the founder of the School of Healing Arts for asking me to teach Breathwork at his school and Veronica Cruz of SOHA for asking me to teach pranayama in their Yoga Teacher Training program.

My appreciation goes out to massage schools, the International College of Holistic Studies and Healing Hands School of Holistic Studies that have included Breathwork in their curriculum. I am also thankful to the National Certification Board for Therapeutic Massage and Bodywork NCBTMB for recognizing Breathwork for continuing education credits/units. I am now certified to offer 12 CEUs.

I am grateful to Tah Groen with Healing Touch Vinyasa for contacting me out of the blue or Facebook to teach in her Yoga Teacher Training in La Jolla.

I am grateful to my friends and colleagues that took the time to help proofread, edit and give feedback on this material. Thank you Megan Allen, Tah Groen, Kylea Taylor, Catherine Dowling, Bruce McArthur, Amy Berg, Patricia Brennon and others you know who you are. Thank you!

I thank you for your time, energy and curiosity in this writing and thank you for your interest in pranayama, Breathwork and the breath, the key ingredient to life on this planet, the invisible connection we all share.

I want to thank you for letting my words and art (the cover) into your mind and possibly your heart. Welcome to a written piece of my world and ongoing journey with breath.

Thank you!

The breath is the vital force

that sustains our life

as we know it now.

With that in mind,

being able to direct this force

is a key to unlocking our full

potential. ©

James Beard

Foreword

When I hear a yoga teacher say they teach Breathwork, I cringe just a little these days and take a conscious breath and smile. It's a start. The Breathworker in me has become patient with such statements and has set his pride aside.

When I was first inspired by western yoga to teach the difference between pranayama and Breathwork my rough draft title read: Pranayama vs Breathwork. I can be very competitive and aggressive at times.

In this corner, we have the western light weight on the average two minute pranayama verses the one to three hour conscious connected breathing heavy weight Breathwork.

There is a big difference between the two. And I don't want our western culture to think western yoga breathing exercises are Breathwork. They are usually a short sample of the fourth limb of yoga, pranayama.

In my five hundred plus hours of yoga training only a very small percentage was devoted to pranayama. I changed my view after I personally dove into the depth of pranayama, and disciplined myself with a daily practice over the last couple of years. It changed my ignorant attitude from "verses" to "and" and I softened my approach with a new understanding, experience and appreciation of the ancient art of pranayama.

I love my breath. It has been one of my main entertainments since I was a small child. Even in the middle years of my life, conscious breathing exercises are still revealing sub or super conscious pieces of my total self (inner and outer).

As I breathed each of the following pranayamas for a minimum of forty-five minutes, without much expectation (because of my curled up nose towards pranayama), my ego was caught off guard. It had learned how to defend itself against my regular Breathwork practices keeping its-small-self intact. The extended pranayama practice was surprisingly pleasant and gave me a new appreciation for the power of our breath.

It is my hope that this workbook shines a loving light on the wonderful practice of conscious breathing and the healthy benefits pranayama and Breathwork have to offer.

Enjoy the journey.

Life is an adventure with a wide variety of experience and choice.

PS This workbook is a guide that is taught with an experiential workshop. Hopefully it is also an inspiration for you to have your very own conscious connected breathing experience because it found a way into your life outside of a yoga studio.

Author's Preface

As I edited some of the pranayama and Breathwork material written on the following pages I was on a cleansing fast. I combined all the different cleanses I have done in the past into one fluid cleanse. It started with a day of raw food after a weekend of burgers and beer. Then a day of veggies and fruit smoothies (blender), to a day of fresh veggie juice (juicer), to two days of the masters cleanse (lemonade diet for some) complete with salt water flushes, to San Diego alkaline filtered water for a day, to two days of breath only. Yes, just breathing. It was interesting to witness how much of my day revolved around eating food. Then back to a day of Alkaline88 water (it tasted sweet and plasticky) and pure coconut water (ahh!) (I could not, and would not, drink the San Diego filtered water, something about it felt wrong and sickening), to another day of fresh juice, then back to the blender, a day of smoothies and veggie broth. Then gentle raw food for a day and back to searching the cupboards and fridge for something easy and tasty to eat.

I explore and practice what I teach. I write from a personal point of view. I share from my experience and perception that is sometimes altered by the power of conscious breathing. I examine myself, each part of my being in the following categories: body, mind, heart, energy and spirit in a way to understand what I am. I practice. I encourage you, the reader, the student, the curious, the explorer of inner self and life outside to have your own experience. Create an adventure with your life and conscious breathing into the depths of what you are and who you have become.

In the world of yoga I know here in the west, the standard practice for pranayama is as follows with variations of course:

- Sit or lie comfortably.
- Inhale slowly.
- Do X amount of rounds (a few minutes tops).
- Rest.
- Repeat.
- Witness, notice the difference before and after the pranayama.

The traditionally claimed benefits of pranayama and proper efficient breathing are across the board. I am listing some of them here from my reading research on pranayama to cut down on writing redundancy with each pranayama.

> According to some studies, you can inhale and exhale up to seven times as much air with proper efficient breathing.

Benefits (Traditionally Claimed Possible)
The Why:

- Relieves tension, anger and anxiety
- Effective for people suffering from hypertension as it calms down the agitated mind
- Gives relief if you're feeling hot or have a slight headache
- Helps mitigate migraines
- Improves memory
- Builds confidence
- Helps in reducing blood pressure
- Makes the voice pleasant and melodious
- Heals diseases of the throat
- Counters shyness
- Stretches the throat and neck, moving lymph for detoxification
- Cools the body
- Heals acidity
- Relieves indigestion and disorders of the bile
- Improves health of eyes and skin
- Heals tonsillitis
- Releases emotion
- Relieves tension in the chest and face
- Strengthens vocal cords
- Refines the breath and awareness of prana flow (I like this)
- Calms the body
- Focuses the mind helping to remove distractions making it easier to concentrate and meditate

Breathe on an empty stomach.

Precautions
The Why Not:

- Never strain the breath in pranayama.
- Do not engage in pranayama right after eating a meal.
- If you are pregnant practice equalizing the inhale and exhale without the retentions.
- If you have high blood pressure, lung, heart, eye or ear problems it's advised not to hold the breath after the inhale.
- If you have low blood pressure it's advised not to hold the breath after the exhale.

Some of the written research I found in books, on Google and Wiki share the possible benefits and healings pranayama is good for. For more of this information type 'Pranayama' in your favorite search engine. To have the experience yourself, start consciously breathing today. *Create a daily practice.* Trust yourself, trust your body, your feelings, your spirit and witness the mind because it has been infiltrated in a sense and not always with the most productive of teachings or examples. And, if I don't mention this next part I would not be doing this wonderful work justice.

Fear! It is sometimes disguised as control.

Some yoga teachers teach fear around the practice of pranayama. I recommend you respect your limits, your boundaries and the dissection of yourself when you apply this practice in your life. Do not do as I do unless you feel totally comfortable and confident. Be courageous, you may relive the deepest, darkest hidden aspects of your false self. Be the courageous, confident, innocent and committed discoverer of the true self and breathe lovingly through the veils of misperception into the worthy truth.

For example, one of the writings on the Web states, "Hold your breath as long as possible." What does that mean? Until you are uncomfortable! Until you pass out! As long as possible, my most recent recorded stagnant hold time was four minutes thirty-two seconds (4:32) long. At the end of Ujjayi pranayama my non-stagnant hold was two minutes (2:00). As I held my breath I went to the bathroom and checked the mail while timing it. The question I pose is, "what is the intention of holding?" You will find those answers in the deep end of yoga somewhere deep down in Samadhi (a level of meditation) where you are not holding your breath. You simply don't need to breathe. Because you are connected to the principle source of life, the spirit of it all, in a state of breathlessness, the true dead man's pose, Savasana.

Each of the following pranayamas I practiced for a minimum of forty-five minutes. Keep in mind this is not common in the western world of yoga I know and that I was a Breathworker long before I became certified in yoga. Under the influence of each pranayama's uniqueness, I would start writing my experience in an altered state, frequency or vibration of myself. Most of the time continuing breathing the pranayama I was writing about and sometimes just disappearing in meditation. Each pranayama had its own flavor of experience and phenomena, from purely physical sensations to highly emotional healing and spiritual perception with deep understanding and insight.

I hope you enjoy this writing, part of my experience and that you are inspired to start a practice of your own. Invite friends and students to join you. Remember to trust yourself, your gut, your intuition, what you feel. Be the witness not the judge.

Namaste

From the divine in me,

to the divine in you.

Contents

Pranayamas

Breathwork

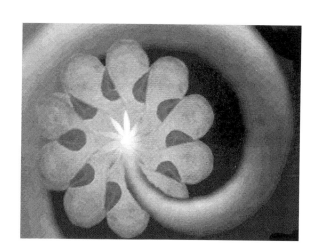

A student of the great Indian poet Kabir

Once asked him,

"Kabir, where is God?"

His answer was simple:

"God is the breath within the breath."

❖   ❖   ❖

Let us really learn how to breathe,

God.

Pranayama is among the most mystified aspects of yoga.

Mark Stephens

Breathe

Pranayama

Prana = Life force energy, breath

Yama = control, mastery, liberation, work

Or

Pran = Life

Ayama = Way

The finest manifestation of prana is thought.

Raja Yoga

If you can't breathe or you are not conscious of your breath
in a pose, is it beneficial to you, your body or your student?

Om
(A u m...)

Om has been discussed and written about over the centuries by many teachers, all sharing their view of the appropriate way to do this chant. I find chanting Om to be one of the best ways to bring a group of people together, to unite them in the moment. I also know that Om is chanted or sung on the average three times at the beginning or end of a yoga class. (One round in the yoga world I know.) When I chanted Om for forty-five minutes to an hour I noticed more of the subtleties of this wonderful pranayama. When I relaxed into it and let the sound drop down into my body, (out of my head and mind) my body started to vibrate and resonate throughout. I felt very, very clear afterwards.

Some have written in the beginning there was nothing and out of the nothingness there came sound. Some have written in the beginning out of the nothingness came light. I say, "I know nothing. I teach nothingness. And I want to take you to a place with no name." We were there, you and I. It is just a matter of remembering, like remembering our birth, possible but not easy. I believe sound and light came at the same time. There was probably a smell of ozone, a taste of some kind and a sensation as consciousness, intelligence and life started to take form and organize.

Some write this original sound is called Spanda. And for some Spanda is defined as the tremor of the heart. I personally like this definition. The vibration of this first sound divided the nothingness into two opposing forces. In the vibration of this original sound the whole universe exists in the field of these contrasting powers. It is written if the sound fades into silence, then the universe will disintegrate again into nothingness. I believe this is why our little egos can't sit still for too long in silence, there is nothing to identify them.

Tantra philosophy describes the whole cosmos as a temporary dance between two opposing forces, ascending energy (Prana) and descending energy (Apana), inhalation and exhalation, male and female, light and dark, hard and soft, positive and negative, sun and moon, destroying and procreating, igniting and grounding, Uddiyana Bandha and Mula Bandha, deconstruction and reconstruction. Enjoy the dance, the balance of being both and conspire.

Udgeeth

Chanting Om

How to:

1. Sit in a comfortable relaxed posture, or stand, dance, etc. Find what works best for you.
2. In this pranayama the inhaling is full and the exhaling duration is long and drawn out.
3. Inhale deeply and while exhaling chant Ommmmmmmmm (aaaauuuummmm....) for a long time slowly bringing the lips together into the hum of the M sound and the silence completing the exhale through the nose clearing the lungs of air.
4. Repeat this for five to ten minutes or more to really explore it.
5. Then sit within the silence of your mind, being and blessing of Om.

Udgeeth (pronounced ood- gee-th) is also known as "Omkari Japa" which means chanting of "Om." Udgeeth pranayama is a simple breathing exercise and recommended to be practiced daily.

Why:

- It calms the mind and brings stability.
- It relieves tension, anger and anxiety.
- Excellent breathing exercises for meditation.

  Some people claim the following.

- It heals problems related to sleep (Insomnia), bad dreams, the nervous system and acidity.
- Reduces high blood pressure.
- Improves memory.

Trust yourself

Questions for each Pranayama

Were the directions clear?

Were you comfortable?

Would props have helped with your comfort?

How would you teach this pranayama? Add or take away.

Practice teaching three times out loud by yourself or with a partner.

How did that feel?

What would you change?

Personal Practice: At least fifteen minutes. What did you experience?

Physically

Mentally

Emotionally

Energetically

Spiritually

When would you use this Pranayama?

Ujjayi

I like the spelling of this pranayama
known here in the west as the

Victorious or Ocean's Breath

How to:

1. Sit in a comfortable relaxed posture or combine with an asana.
2. Constrict the back of your mouth (epiglottis), while inhaling and exhaling through your nose, similar to quiet snoring.
3. Place the tip of your tongue on the roof of your mouth just behind your front teeth.

Ujjayi (pronounced ew-gy-eee) is one of the most popular pranayamas combined with asana, the physical practice of yoga. Ujjayi makes an audible breath that is often compared to the sound of the ocean, hence the name. With the constriction of the upper throat, the Ujjayi breath streams in and out through the nostrils with the lips remaining gently closed. From my experience it can be done in hatha yoga (slow, detailed, fewer postures) where I took note of an average and equal count, four inhales and exhales per pose. When I switched to Vinyasa flow yoga (faster, aerobic, more poses) the count changed to an average count of two.

My Experience:

This breath is easily maintained throughout a yoga practice or doing chores around the house. I found vacuuming to be a little challenging because I couldn't hear myself. But I could feel it. I also found writing and critical thinking to be a challenge while trying to maintain this pranayama.

When I lied down to breathe Ujjayi my ears started to ring (tinnitus). This pranayama also never warmed my body as it has been written and I have heard some yoga teachers say it is a warming breath.

I breathed the Ujjayi for over an hour while I did some yoga and chores. Around the thirty-five minute mark I sat still with it outside for ten minutes, eyes closed to focus on this pranayama. I felt unnecessary tension in my jaw and relaxed it. Then I tuned into my body with the question; "What else can I relax?" I noticed only my lower diaphragm being activated. My chest was barely moving unless I drew out the inhale. That didn't feel productive in the stillness. Near the end of ten minutes of stillness doing Ujjayi my breath took on a life of its own. I just witnessed it and found it joyfully interesting. I held the breath for a moment and felt a rush of energy making me light-headed like standing up too quickly and went into a short meditation before writing.

When I sat down to write I spontaneously asked my body for forgiveness, overwhelmed with gratitude for all the experiences I have put it through and been through with it. I asked my body for forgiveness and promised to be a better host. It was like I had an out of body in body experience. I, my spiritual self, recognized the intelligence and animal my body is. This was quite a loving, with tears in my eyes response. In that sense of Ujjayi I felt victorious. I felt my body loves me like a dog loves its master. And like a dog it will eat and do as it pleases if it is not disciplined but loves you unconditionally either way. I know I am not this body and I forget this knowing. I am something far greater--eternal--so I choose to enjoy my body, this gift while it lasts. And when I truly discipline it and ultimately raise its vibration, I believe I can take it with me back into the cosmos. The masters have and so can we; it is just a matter of continuing to peel away the layers, the beliefs hiding the truth of what and who we are.

Pause

Breathe

Bhramari
The Bee's Breath

How to:

1. Make yourself comfortable and gently smile.
2. Keep your back straight, shoulder muscles relaxed and eyes closed.
3. Gently close both your ears with your index fingers or thumbs _using the ear cartilage_.
4. Raise your elbows to the level of your shoulders out to your sides.
5. Inhale deeply.
6. Retain your breath for a moment or two.
7. Exhale slowly making a buzzing sound, like that of a bee. You can make a low-pitched sound or a high one. Play with it for best results. Even separate your teeth a little to fluctuate the vibration.
8. Breathe in again and continue the same pattern six to seven times or more.
9. Relax your arms and the breath.
10. Keep your eyes closed for some time. Observe the sensations in the body and quietness within. Be the witness.

I suggest trying it any time of the day that you could use some peace and quiet.

Bhramari (pronounced bra-mar-eee) is very effective in instantly calming down and clearing your mind. It is simple to do and can be practiced anywhere to de-stress and refocus yourself. This breathing technique derives its name from the black Indian bee called Bhramari. The exhalation in this pranayama resembles the typical humming sound of a bee, which explains the name.

My Experience:

With this pranayama my shoulders became tired quickly, part to do with the fasting and part to do with not ever practicing this position for forty-five minutes. I played with the quality of tone and how my body emotionally responded to it. I have an app on my smart phone titled DaTuner Lite. I found the note of F3 to feel the best for me. G3 was a natural note. C3 was when I felt bored with the exercise and the momentary despair when I caught the lazy part of myself thinking, I would be doing all of the following pranayamas for forty-five minutes to go deep into the experience of them.

I did this practice upon awakening at 5:30 in the morning on the second day of my fast with no food or water (to put this in some sort of context). I found having my fingers holding my ears closed to be limiting and distracting for this length of time. I moved into child pose to relieve the weight of my arms.

This is when I felt the vibrations of Bhramari soften my body deeper into the surrender of this pose. My body and mind had adjusted to the lower volume of humming and the mental chatter started up again at twenty-four minutes. I put more effort into Bhramari increasing the volume of the bee sound and my mind became clear once again. At thirty minutes I started to burp much to my surprise as I had not eaten food for over forty-eight hours. I concluded with fifteen minutes of silence and felt very peaceful.

Take a slow inhale and exhale.

When would you use the pranayama?

At the beginning of a class maybe.

Practice, until it is sweet like honey.

Simhasana

Lion's Breath/Pose

How to:

1. Sit comfortably or kneel, buttocks on your heels with your hands and knees on the floor.
2. Inhale stretching your head up and arching it back.
3. Exhale with tongue out and down towards the chin while roaring out a loud "HA."
4. Open eyes focused between the eyebrows (drishti), cross-eyed, looking up.
5. Relax your head, neck, shoulders and spine back to neutral for a natural breath.
6. Repeat for a couple of rounds.

Simhasana (pronounced sim-ha-sah-nah) 'Simha' means 'Lion' and 'asana' means 'pose'. This pranayama resembles a seated lion roaring.

My Experience:

I cannot write I sounded like a lion. I sounded more like an angry or scared man expressing himself. (I will get confirmation from my neighbors☺.) I actually moved to the back room of my house so no one would come over to ask if I was alright. Before this exercise I felt resistance to get started but once I started it felt good.

I sat in a chair for the first ten minutes and then moved to my yoga mat in a kneeling posture. I crossed my feet both ways but preferred them next to each other. Thirty minutes in, I moved to table pose on my hands and knees for the inhale and exhaled at the peak in cow pose, arching my back down and my head up and back. I concluded on my knees in a meditative kneeling pose (Bhujrasana).

In the beginning my focus on drishti was in and out. I also found folding and stretching my neck forward and down after three or four rounds helped with my comfort. Twenty minutes in, I spontaneously started circling my neck and increased the volume of my lion's roar that sounded like a drawn out "HAAAA!!!" I noticed the emotion of anger in my tone and brought a joyful emotion to the feeling of my expression and tone. I tried other emotions too for personal experience. I put so much force into the sound, like I had been startled or scared and burst out a short, "HA!" that some of the metal objects in my room started to ring.

The pause or natural breath in between each roar took me into a brief meditative state with my eyes focused on my third eye (drishti) and the tip of my tongue naturally placed on the roof of my mouth while sitting in a relaxed kneeling posture. And of course I slipped into a daydream or two forgetting the exercise, my intention and where my body was for a moment or more, which finally led me into thoughts bringing me back to the exercise. I started pulling the energy of my breath up my spine as my neck extended and arched back to release the climatic "HA!" for several rounds at a time.

It was then I noticed a small column of white light coming into my head unintentionally. I turned Simhasana into a healing practice, letting this loving light flood and permeate my body's cells on the pause breath in between roars. I drew in more of this vibrant healing energy with each next inhale while emotionally releasing old cellular memory, dis-ease, dis-comfort and thoughts to a ball of blue-white light energy at the top of my throat. I exhaled with powerful intuitive natural emotion with the intention to purify my body, mind and soul. Pleasantly surprised once again by the healing and spiritual power of breath I vibrated in the joyful silence with my heart full of gratitude.

When I finally stood in awe and thanks, I felt very light-headed. I have only experienced this practice briefly in my yoga training and in one or two yoga classes for only one or two rounds. If you use this pranayama during your yoga practice set aside your inhibitions about what you may look and sound like and just let it out. You may surprise yourself like I did.

Another why:

Simhasana helps keep the platysma firm as we age, tighten the neck skin, so it has been written. Practice and prove it to be truth, aka real.

Just go for it, play!

Have fun.

Let go.

SHEETALI
Cooling Breath

How to:

1. Sit in a comfortable relaxed posture.
2. Close your eyes and relax your whole body with normal breathing
3. Put your tongue across the lower lip and try to roll your tongue edges up making a tube to breathe through.
4. Inhale deeply through the tongue tube.
5. Close your mouth and retain/hold your breath until the cool feeling fades.
6. Slowly exhale through the nose.

This is one round of Sheetali pranayama. Do as many as you need to cool or feel comfortable. Trust yourself.

Why not:

This pranayama is not recommended during winter, for people prone to being cold, or suffering from a heavy cold.

Sheetali ((Shitali alternate spelling) pronounced she-tall-eee) is a pranayama designed to help you regulate the body's heat. It is recommended to only do this breath in the summer or after a vigorous or heated practice like Bikram. The suggested rounds vary per instructor and I happen to find that quite entertaining.

My Experience:

My house was sixty eight-degrees when I started the in-depth practice of Sheetali for forty-five minutes. After about ten minutes I started to get a slight headache at my third eye. My longest retention was thirty seconds and I averaged about fifteen second retentions throughout. I had a conversation with the pain in my forehead and third eye area asking, "What is going on?" Shorter retention was the answer and then I started having visions, some led into daydreams where I lost Sheetali but most were enjoyable as they passed before my inner eye. I found a pausing breath in between the curled tongue breaths, helped too.

Somewhere part way into this pranayama my lazy voice spoke up, "You don't need to do forty-five minutes of this pranayama, nobody will know." I responded, "I will" and continued to breathe. During this practice, my gut developed gas which I found interesting because once again I was not eating at that time. I never did cool down which was a concern before I started because it was the tail end of winter 2016.

To be honest I have never used Sheetali to cool my body down. I take cold showers for that. But try it and see if it works for you.

Take a moment here to really practice one of the following pranayamas and write a short note about your experience.

Ugeedth

Ujjayi

Bhramari

Simhasana

Sheetali

SHEETKARI
Hissing Breath

How to:

1. Sit in a meditative pose or in a comfortable posture on the floor.
2. Keep the back straight and shoulders relaxed.
3. Place hands on the knees, fingers relaxed and eyes closed.
4. Join lower and upper teeth.
5. Fix the front portion of the tongue against the front teeth and the rest of the tongue on the palate, the roof of your mouth.
6. Separate the lips and inhale from the mouth making a hissing or "I am cold" sound.
7. Retain your breath for a few moments or until the coolness fades.
8. Exhale through both nostrils.

This is one round of Sheetkari pranayama.

Sheetkari ((Shitkari alternate spelling) pronounced she-car-eee) is pranayama intended to cool the body similar to Sheetali Pranayama and is suggested to be done after practicing asanas or other pranayamas for its cooling effect. I did not practice this pranayama after practicing any asanas or after another pranayama.

My Experience:

I started at 8:10 am and ten to fifteen minutes in, I started dozing into a slump on the retention part. My hands became very cold (my house was sixty four degrees at the time of this practice) so I sat on them. I would come out of my doze and continue the practice. I focused on my third eye and had flashes of light and dreamy visions. Upon what seemed like a longer doze I thought I should start this practice over to give it a genuine forty-five minutes. I checked the time it was precisely 8:55am. I tell my students sometimes sleep is the necessary practice and recognized it for myself and felt my truthful experience was the appropriate way to share my forty-five minute practice of Sheetkari.

Those who find it difficult to do Sheetali Pranayama can easily practice Sheetkari and get similar benefits.

I have left these benefits here because I found one to be contradictive to my personal experience and the other beneficial and promising.

Why:

- According to Hatha Yoga Pradeepika, Sheetkari removes hunger, thirst, sleep and lassitude (my contradiction).
- Sheetkari is good for the health of your teeth and gums. (I like this because I feel the air being pulled through my teeth and along my gums. And at this time in my life I am getting long in the tooth.)

Why not:
Avoid this pranayama if you suffer from low blood pressure (cold hands?).

Take a note for yourself, what is in agreement with you and what is not.

Knowledge is not experience.

Breathe

Nadi Shodhana
Alternate Nostril Breathing

The following methods are variations of Nadi Shodhana.

CHANDRABHEDAN

How to:

1. Sit in a meditative pose or in a comfortable position on the floor.
2. Keep your back straight and shoulders relaxed.
3. Close your right nostril with right hand thumb.
4. Inhale from the left nostril.
5. Close the left nostril with the right hand index and middle fingers.
6. Exhale from the right nostril.
   This completes one round of Chandrabhedan pranayama. Increase the rounds up to the recommended 20 rounds over time.

Why:

Chandrabhedan cools the body and cures heartburn.

Why not:
Avoid this pranayama if you suffer from low blood pressure.

This pranayama is to be done only during summer.

SURYABHEDAN

How to:

1. Sit in a meditative pose or in a comfortable posture.
2. Close your left nostril with your index and middle finger of the right hand.
3. Inhaling from your right nostril.
4. Close the right nostril with your right hand thumb.
5. Exhale through the left nostril.
   This completes one round of Suryabhedan pranayama. Increase the rounds up to the recommended 20 rounds over time.

Why:

- Increases body heat and energy levels
- Improves digestion

- Purifies blood
- Delays ageing

Why not:

- Avoid doing this pranayama if you suffer from acidity, hypertension or heart problems.
- It is to be done only during winter.

ANULOM-VILOM

How to:

1. Sit in a comfortable balanced meditative pose.
2. Use your right-hand thumb to close your right nostril.
3. Inhale from the left nostril.
4. Close your left nostril with your right hand's index and middle fingers
5. Exhale from the right nostril.
6. Do the reverse: inhale with the right nostril.
7. Close your right nostril with your right-hand thumb.
8. Exhale with the left nostril.
   This is one round of anulom-vilom pranayama.

Why:

- Balances body temperature
- Relieves stress
- Cleanses the nadis in your body
- Improves blood circulation
- Promotes longevity

It can be done year-round and by everyone.

There are many versions of right/left nostril breathing and it is referenced in my book, Thirteen Breaths to Freedom. When I wrote that book, I had given up on this subtle practice, which I understand a lot more of today. In my previous writing I was recalling from memory my little experience with Nadi Shodhana. Back in the day I was only breathing the physical part of this breath not the mental, subtle, energetic, sensing part of the breath. In other words I was not moving the nadi energy with my mind, will and intention.

My Experience:

Today I directed my attention to the nadis of my spine. The Ida, cooling left side, the Pingala, warming right side and the Shashumna, the balance between the two which in turn has the *potential* to release dormant energy in my root chakra known as Kundalini. This potentially rises up my spine opening all of my Chakras on its ascent.

In my regular morning practice I only do a few rounds of Nadi Shodhana but today I dedicated my practice to this pranayama. I did ten rounds of Chandrabhedan and ten of Suryabhedan with a normal breath in between. Then I started breathing a version of Nadi Shodhana to a count of six for the inhale, held for twenty four, exhaled for twelve. (This is a 1-4-2, multiplier I suggest starting with 4-16-8 or 3-12-6)

I visualized the energy of the Nadi I was breathing spiraling around the first six chakras from the root to the third eye. I kept my eyes closed and focused on the space between my eye brows, (drishti). When I relaxed from several rounds of Nadi Shodhana I would breathe, visualize and intend moving the dormant energy straight up my spine to my third eye. I also found it more productive not to count just breathe and retain the breath with comfort so I was not in my head but in my body and senses.

In these moments I realized an old fear was still within me. "I was afraid of God." This feeling came up as the light flashed upon my third eye. Part of my being was not ready to surrender completely. My little ego was hanging on, hanging on to my name and the things that identify James: the knowns, people, places and possessions. In this moment of recognition I noticed another part of me that believes in a punishing God taking me back to my very young days in a Christian-based family. I did my best to let go of these false beliefs and resonate with my following truth:

A gentle loving voice in my head said, "You will dissolve back into me, into me one day, it is inevitable. Why not do it consciously, now?" I released my fear and smiled at the truth of these words I heard and knew in my head, but not completely in my heart. I love and respect the power of God, not the one I was taught by others, but the one I have come to know with such practices as these pranayamas. It has been quite a challenge to step out of the cultural mindset into the truth I have come to know and what I believe is true. Even in the editing of this piece my heart spontaneously opened and tears of happiness flooded my eyes. I am so grateful in this moment.

If these words resonate as truth to you, I wish you the best in releasing your subconscious cellular beliefs and mindset. May you start your daily practice and enjoy your journey to remembering our collective human truth, we are all one.

There is subtleness to the practice of pranayama that takes time and devotion.

Are you willing to put in the time?

Are you willing to devote part of your day to pranayama?

Are you ready to take a good look at yourself?

Physically

Mentally

Emotionally

Energetically

Spiritually

Sama Vritti
Equal Breathing

Some write the purpose of this pranayama is to equalize four components of breathing.

Inhalation (puraka)   Internal retention (antara-khumbaka)

Exhalation (rechaka)   External retention (bahya-khumbaka)

How to:

1. Sit comfortably, your spine upright.
2. Spend a few minutes watching your natural breath.
3. Begin with an exhale for a count of four.
4. Hold the exhale out for a count of four.
5. Inhale for a count of four.
6. Hold the inhale in for a count of four.
7. After a few rounds take the count up keeping the count equal on all four parts.

You can stay at 4 or if you find you are struggling with the breath simply lower it to 2 or 3 until it feels easier. Cultivate the same quality of each breath at the beginning, middle and end of the count. Do not be force or strain the breath during this pranayama. After several rounds sit and observe how you feel.

Beginners can practice without the retentions just equalize the inhale and exhale.

Sama Vritti (pronounced saw-mah-veert-tee) an alternate spelling is Samavritti. Sama translates as equal, even, smooth and Vritti translates as whirlpool, fluctuations, waves and ripples referring to a mental state that pranayama can help balance.

My Experience:

I normally do a few progressive rounds of this pranayama. I start at two, then four, then eight, then sixteen, and then thirty-two. My goal is to complete a sixty-four count round. For this publication I did several of the above progressions (2,4,8,16,32) while visualizing a square. Then the following happened.

I naturally started breathing the inhale up, belly to chest, hold, front to back, exhale down the back, retention back to front for a count of two with a Natural-Rhythm-Breath (NRB) in-between rounds. I changed to a four-count visualizing slightly expanded square with political thoughts passing through my mind. NRB Then I changed. I changed to a five-count only progressing by one with a little more expansion of my square and it started rotating; breathing up the front, retaining front to back, exhaling down the back, retaining back to front and so on. I watched my concentration start to slip in the retentions. I was counting the visualized square still within the torso with thoughts of, save the world vibe and if you haven't saved yourself how are you going to save the world? NRB Next was a six-count that naturally turned into breathing from the root chakra to my third eye. I inhaled six-count up the front of my body, mentally energizing each chakra area, holding my breath at the focal point of my third eye for six and then exhaled down the back side of the chakra points counting to six a holding of my breath for another six-count at the base chakra. My mind was clear and focused.

The seven-count was nearly the same as six but I recognized the square had become a tight oval with the retention in the crown and base chakras. I did two rounds of seven-count then NRB in between.

The eight-count was similar to seven at the count of eight I felt the etheric field all around my torso and head; alive, almost goose bumpy, energized holding my attention there. Then I exhaled down through my chakra points to the base and on the retention my diaphragm started sending signals to breathe as I focused on the energy permeating my body. NRB

The nine-count was the same breathing up through the chakras with my attention on the mental field around my head at the count of nine, retention for nine and exhaling down my back to a count of nine. My diaphragm adjusted. I felt very clear and did two rounds.

The tenth was the same, but I stopped counting and just felt the points of interest up and out of my body, through and beyond my etheric and mental field to an emotional area within my energetic body. I felt subtle joy as I was no longer counting but feeling the equality and quality of inhaling in a line up my body, holding my breath in this space, exhaling down my body and holding my breath out with awareness and joy.

The eleven-count breath took me to points of interest in my extremities, especially my legs and hands. The twelve-count breath included all the previous fields and expanded to the inside edge of my astral field. It was like exploring my aura, the circle of energy around my body and presence as I felt and sensed through my third eye. It looked like a little white shimmer of light. I was feeling really good at this point.

The thirteen-breath count I went beyond, beyond my conscious self, simply expanded and stayed there in meditation for a while. The forty-five minutes I dedicated to this pranayama was up but there was no point to leave this meditation. Later in the day when I went out into the world I had a smile for everyone I met, energized with compassion, patience and completeness. I was pleasantly surprised by this pranayama, as I have been with most of them so far and I recognized a common theme. I am doing them all for at least forty-five minutes minimum and I have dropped my attitude.

Dirga Swasam

Three Part Breath

How to:

1. Sit comfortably or lie down.
2. Start with breathing into your belly, several rounds.
3. Relax to normal breathing.
4. Breathe into your upper chest for several rounds.
5. Relax to normal breathing.
6. Now breathe into your heart, the center of your chest, the center of your being, expanding in all directions simultaneously.
7. Relax to normal breathing.
8. Breathe deep into the lower belly back bringing the breath to upper belly through the heart and on up into the upper chest filling in under your collar bones, stretching yourself from the inside out.

Dirga Swasam (pronounced deer-gah-swha-sahm) is a good pranayama for new yogis and teachers. The full name comes from two Sanskrit words. "Dirga" (also spelled "Deerga") has several meanings, including "slow," "deep," "long," and "complete." I don't agree with complete and you'll know why as you continue applying the practices within these pages and learn about the Micro Cosmic Orbit. "Swasam" refers to the breath. Therefore, this practice is sometimes also referred to as "Complete Breath." It is also often simply called "Dirga Pranayama."

My Experience:

This morning's dawn I awoke and started the day with Dirga Swasam lying down. I breathed deep into my belly from my pubic bone to bottom of my sternum for a couple of rounds. Then I breathed into my upper chest as I teach it to others, expanding so the shoulders naturally moved back. Then I breathed into my heart, the center of my body behind the sternum expanding in all directions, front to back, side to side, up and down for a couple of rounds.

Then I put it all together from my pubic bone slowly up under my clavicles and slowly exhaled. I noticed the title "Three Part Breath," seemed to be up in my head, flat in my mind, compartmentalized: one belly, two heart, three chest. Noticing this, I got out of my head and felt the breath move my belly down and out and then up under my sternum with continued expansion starting between my low ribs and on up my chest into the bottom of my throat. This felt much smoother than one, two, three and more relaxing.

In this state I felt the pranic expansion of my cells, the electric tingling sensation throughout and around my body. I could hear the birds start to sing their morning call to life, outside my window, and I remembered a breathwork message from a while ago: "Raise the vibration of your bones" as I watched a vision of a blue skeleton dance inside a misty white whirl wind.

After that recollection the electric vibration went further into my body lighting up my skeletal system. My breathing would naturally suspend, stopping in the stillness of this higher frequency of being. In there, in that space, that moment, there was no need to breathe. Just be and enjoy the love within.

I felt my nerve plexuses and witnessed the energy move with the direction of my mind. I also noticed how my mind would affect my breathing when it drifted off eagerly trying to file my new experience into a known category with no success. Random thoughts of the past or the day to come would briefly distract my breath connection to this blissful state and once caught, were easily brought back into the perfect space of meditation and higher vibration. I found this energetic, vibrant-*actuality* to be very loving, healing and comforting.

This is my wish for everyone I meet.

Take a moment here to really practice one of the following pranayamas and write a short note about your experience.

Sheetkari

Nadi Shodhana

Sama Vriti

Dirga Swasam

Kapalabhati

Skull Shining

How To:

1. Sit comfortable where your spine is straight and your abdomen not compressed.
2. Rest your hands on your knees, palms facing down.
3. Bring your awareness to your lower belly. To heighten your awareness, you can place your hands, one on top of the other, on your lower belly rather than on your knees.
4. Inhale through both nostrils deeply.
5. Contract your low belly or use your hands to gently press on this area, forcing out the breath in a short burst. Your focus should be on exhaling.
6. As you quickly release the contraction, inhale naturally and effortlessly.
7. Begin slowly, with one breath per second. Gradually quicken the pace, aiming for 100 exhalation/inhalation cycles per minute. Always go at your own pace and stop if you feel faint or dizzy.
8. After one minute of the exercise, inhale deeply through the nostrils, and then exhale slowly through your mouth. Depending on your experience level, you may repeat the exercise.

Trust yourself

The name is from two Sanskrit words: "Kapala" meaning "skull" and "Bhati" meaning "light."

This is why it is sometimes referred to as "Shining Skull, Light Skull Breathing" or "Skull Brightener Breath" depending of course upon the teacher or writer informing you. As you practice Kapalabhati you can have a personal understanding of the name yourself.

Kapalabhati (also spelled Kapalbhati) (pronounced kah-pah-luh-bah-tee) consists of short, powerful exhales and relaxed inhales. This pranayama is known by some as a traditional internal purification practice that tones and cleanses the respiratory system by encouraging the release of toxins. It has refreshed and rejuvenated many a body, mind and soul.

Practicing Kapalabhati can bring balance and purity to your life on many levels, including physical, mental, emotional, energetic and spiritual. Remember to take it slow at first, and build on your experience as you gain more control. Breathing consciously, yet effortlessly, can break down barriers that you didn't even know existed! The benefits of regular pranayama practice will show up in all areas of your life, both on and off the mat. Let's Breathe!

Why:

- Invigorating and warming
- Helps to cleanse the lungs, sinuses, and respiratory system
- Aids in preventing illness and allergies
- Strengthens the diaphragm and abdominal muscles
- Increases your body's oxygen supply
- Stimulates and energizes the brain while preparing it for meditation and work that requires high focus

My Experience:

Traveling tends to disrupt my morning exercises, practices and meditation. The energy of a new place, time zone, people and my lack of will or jet lag lead to mornings of sleeping in. But today I finally woke in the four o'clock hour and started Kapalabhati. I dedicated forty-five minutes to this pranayama. I heard a bird sing its early morning song once and decide it was too early and returned to silence.

I worked my exhale from my low belly pulling it back in towards my spine. It felt like I was rolling my gut flat up the inside of my back and hollowing out the area under my rib cage in a detailed-drawing-in motion even though I was exhaling.

I started slow, very slow and precise really feeling the motion of this conscious exhale ending with an effortless, relaxed inhale. I worked the exhale deliberately noticing the massage my gut was receiving all the way up to my stomach and liver. I witnessed the natural pull of air into my lungs as I released my contracted abs. The first twenty minutes were connected breaths before I took a round of natural breaths.

Then I started to progressively pick up the pace and every couple of minutes held the breath out. This is where the magic is, as I witnessed my third eye come to life with visions of health and brilliant colors.

When I started in the early morning quiet I wasn't sure I would be able to sustain Kapalabhati for forty five minutes but after the half hour mark I lost track of time and space until the early morning commuters and the morning bird songs made their way back into my consciousness. Sometimes there are no words for the experience of pranayama, Breathwork and yoga.

Bhastrika

Bellows Breath

How to:

1. Sit in a meditative pose or a comfortable position on the floor (no chair). I lie down sometimes, because with this breath you may end up there anyway.
2. Keep your back straight and shoulder muscles relaxed.
3. Close the right nostril with your right thumb and bring your right elbow to the level of right shoulder.
4. Close your eyes. Inhale and exhale through left nostril—first slowly, then a little faster.
5. Do the above steps about 20 – 25 times.
6. Take a long breath in, and retain it for as long as possible.
7. Switch nostrils and repeat.

Or:

Breathe through both nostrils progressively speeding up the breath to the hold.

Or:

Inhale moving your arms and open hands straight up above your head, make fists grabbing prana, exhale pull fists down to shoulder height. Repeat with a seamless breath. Progressively speed up the motion and breathe for several invigorating rounds.

Bhastrika (pronounced bah-stree-kah) is often used to energize the body and clear the mind. It is a very mysterious pranayama and not much is known about it. Bhastrika is aimed at keeping the inhalation cycle equal to exhalation. It is a breathing technique through the nose with equal time for inhalation and exhalation, yet making each breath deeper and longer with equal time intervals using more and more force as one progresses through a round or deeper into this pranayama.

It is a pranayama where we accelerate how much prana or life force is coming into our being. With Bhastrika you breathe forcefully in and out accelerating the breath as you go. Pull the pelvic floor up, the belly in and contract the chest on the exhalation. Fill in the belly and upper chest on the inhale. You may feel your spine oscillating. Do it as best you can, as full as you can. After 20 to 100 breaths (or whatever you are comfortable with), take a deep breath in and hold it. Tilt your head forward drawing your chin down toward the chest and chest towards your chin Jālandhara bandha. Explore with different holding times. When you can no longer hold the breath, release your chin lock, exhale and feel the energy moving to the crown of your head and throughout your body.

Why not:

Avoid practicing Bhastrika pranayama if you suffer from hypertension, heart/lung complications or hernia. Weak people with some illness or a low stamina should avoid doing this pranayama too often. It takes energy to build energy. Pace yourself.

My Experience:

Wow, I have now practiced Bhastrika three different times before writing my experience. I have two words: vibrant and clear. Each time I finished Bhastrika I really had nothing to write and this being the third time, I am convinced that this is the way it is. I can describe the sensations in the physical as an all over vibration, hence vibrant; a total body vibration, smooth, ecstatic, clean, pure in a sense and calm. My mind is clear and it really doesn't care to be writing these words at the moment or is that my lazy ego?

Today I have decided this piece needs to be written so a more disciplined piece of my self is writing the mere words to describe the experience that is better *to do* than read about. So put this book down and start breathing.

As described above and here, progressively build upon each breath to a pinnacle holding the inhale and bandha. I recall doing six rounds of this pranayama within the forty-five minute timeline. I really don't remember exactly. I started off slow, feeling the breath open up my low back behind my guts, finding the lowest part of the diaphragm allowing expansion of my lungs lowest lobes. (On my body that area is straight back from my belly button or you can reach around and try to feel your floating ribs or just above your hips. Those muscles you feel as your rib cage curves inward, need to relax, soften and expand to allow this to happen.) Be very mindful and deliberate as you explore the kidney and adrenal area of your body.

Now here is the fun part, don't get too hung up in your head as you speed up the breath. Do your best to make the inhale and exhale equal, full and complete. It is perfectly fine in my world if your spine oscillates, starts waving back and forth as you start forcefully breathing faster and faster and fuller and fuller.

I honestly prefer to do this breath lying down so I can really let myself go.

I have seen this breath in different settings with variations and called different names or titles: The Warrior's Breath from Supreme Science Qi Gong, 100 Breath from Transformational Breathing and Tantric breathing (you can find a variation in the 1969 Woodstock festival documentary).

Bhastrika is one of the most mystifying pranayamas when explored deeply and passionately. Trust yourself, body and heart. Witness the programs of your mind dissolve, leaving you with nothing but truth and innocence. Do you remember what you are truly looking for?

Agniprasana

Breath of Fire

How to:

1. Sit in a comfortable posture with eyes closed or combine with your favorite asana.
2. Elongate your spine upwards, lengthen your neck and slightly tuck your chin.
3. Breathe rapidly through the nose with equal emphasis on the inhale and exhale, like very fast sniffing. Keep the breath shallow, just at the tip of the nose. Proceed at a comfortable pace and establish a steady rhythm. Your chest and diaphragm stay relaxed for the *most part*. Your stomach may pulse with its own in rhythm to your breath. Continue for one minute, one round.

Intermediate:
Perform the breathing at a faster pace. Increase the duration of the exercise to 3 minutes

Advanced:
Build up the pace and power with which you do the breathing and increase the time to 11 minutes.

What is Agniprasana, the 'Breath of Fire'?
Is it Kapalabhati or is it Bhastrika or Agnisara? It is none of these. It comes from Kundalini Yoga. This pranayama is essential to the practice of Kundalini Yoga. The roots of this pranayama are said to be impossible to trace according to Ravi Singh of Kundalini Yoga.

Why:

- Quickly oxygenates your blood, helping the body detoxify and remove waste more effectively
- Builds lung capacity and helps purify the respiratory system
- Generates heat and increases your level of energy by activating the energy flows in your body (nadis)
- Synchronizes your entire system under one rhythm, promoting internal harmony and health
- Balances and strengthens the nervous system
- Magnifies the benefits of exercises (asanas) done in conjunction with this breath
- When done forcefully, the pulsating of the diaphragm massages the internal organs, thus improving the digestive system.

Why not:

- If you feel dizzy when practicing Breath of Fire, stop and substitute normal breathing.
- If you suffer from vertigo, use caution in practicing this breathing exercise.
- If you are menstruating, use long deep breathing.
- Be careful practicing Breath of Fire if you have high blood pressure, heart disease or suffer from stroke, epilepsy, acid or heat related gastric issues, ulcers use caution.

Once again trust yourself.

My Experience:

I have done this pranayama many times over the years. At first I thought I would just write from that time. But as I have reacquainted myself with the other pranayamas for forty-five minutes I thought it best to continue.

So I started breathing Agniprasana at 11:27 AM lightly sniffing at the tip of my nose. My daughter's dog came out of her room to check in on me with a knowing look upon his furry face. I continued the exercise looking back at him without pause and he returned to his pillow. I noticed the kitchen had been neglected for a few days so I started cleaning up the counters and dishes while sniffing away. My sinuses started to become irritated and cool with the beginning signs of a headache. I took a couple of long inhales through my nose and blew it clean. I felt much better after blowing my nose, which in turn had cleaned, moisturized and warmed it. (keep this in mind)

I continued cleaning up the kitchen and thought I could be doing some yoga while practicing this pranayama but felt called to the clean the bathroom too. It was only when part of my chores demanded my undivided attention that I lost focus of this breathing exercise, like scraping a stubborn spot on a drinking glass from one of my smoothies.

I found this breath to be particularly easy so I speeded the sniffing up to challenge myself and I would have to slow back down to maintain the practice with an occasional long inhale.

I went outside for the last fifteen minutes to sit in my meditation chair sniffing away the time. I focused on my third eye while exploring the rhythm of my breath and being enveloped by the life around me, the sounds of neighborhood traffic, warm summer air and sense of time because I had a client at twelve-thirty for a massage appointment.

My thoughts wandered from, how we have lost our instinctual connection to the earth, one of the basic survival traits of any free animal on this planet, to where we are now, housed, taxed, governed and policed (ID'ed).

I continued the short quick sniffing at the tip of my nose with the warm dry dusty grassy air keeping me present in the summer season. At 12:13 I stopped this pranayama with nothing much to report as I had thought it would be by the memories of my past experience. I smile as I write this part because, did I have the experience I had based on past expectation or because that is how it is with this pranayama for me? (Insert Cheshire grin here.)

Take a moment here to really practice one of the following pranayamas and a write short note about your experience.

Kapalabhati

Bhastrika

Agniprasana

Notes

Bandha

Body lock

Bandha (pronounced bond-hah) meaning; bond, arrest, hold, constrict or constraint, is a term for "body lock" in yoga.

These are the four main bandhas I am aware of:

1. **Mula Bandha**   (pronounced moo-lah)
2. **Uddiyana bandha**   (pronounced ooo-dee-ah-nah)
3. **Jalandhara Bandh**a (pronounced jaw-lond-hah-rah)
4. **Maha Bandha**   (pronounced mah-hah)

I have included the bandha section of pranayama here. For an understanding of what they are before we explore the next pranayama, Agnisara. In my Breathwork practice I do something similar to a bandha but as I have researched and experienced over time I have found what I am doing is not really a bandha, but it is similar. The most information I received in my yoga training for bandhas was from a weekend training in Ashtanga Yoga. The following are basic definitions of this practice. (In my workshop you may receive additional handouts.)

Mula Bandha is basically a contraction of the pelvic floor. There are three parts; anus, perineum and genitals. They are worth exploring to see if you can separate them instead of one main contraction, like passing gas without wetting in yourself.

Uddiyana bandha is a contraction of the abdomen: back in and up under the rib cage. Once again it is three parts; low, middle and upper belly.

Jalandhara Bandha is tucking the chin close to the chest, known as a throat or chin lock. Keep your neck straight, forward fold you head, hinging on the axis. Iyengar writes, "to rest the chin in between the collar bones."

Maha Bandha is combining all three of the above. It is known as the great lock.

For more info check out the link below;

http://www.ashtangayoga.info/ashtangayoga/basics/energy-bandha

Other points of interest: Kumbhaka (breath retention) this was mentioned in the equal breathing section, Sama Vritti.

Mudra: (hand gesture) I am including hand gestures here because I believe the mudras and bandhas happened naturally during any one of the pranayama practices back in the day. And then they defined them from self-exploration, inner research and understanding of the nadis and the meridians. Now they have become a symbolic or ritual gesture in Hinduism, Buddhism and today's yoga Facebook posts without the rich deep experience of the origin. If you have experienced tetany in your hands you will have a better understanding of what I am writing and where I am coming from now.

Notes for Agnisara

Agnisara

Fire Breath

How to:

1. Stand with feet double shoulder width apart, knees bent, slightly squatting.
2. Place hands on knees, arms and back straight, torso leaning forward.
3. Exhale from the lowest part of the abdomen, pushing in and rolling abs upward.
4. Natural inhalation, effortless release of abs.
5. Repeat for several rounds.

Options:

6. You can also do this in bridge pose (Setu Bandha Sarvangasana).
7. Retain breath out with the Jalandhara Bandha, throat lock and continue contracting and rolling the abs up and down and around the gut.

It is said, if in a given day you do not do any other physical exercise, do this practice.

Agnisara (pronounced ag-knee-sar-ah) 'Agni' means 'Fire' and Sara' means "Essence".

My Experience:

I have to admit I wasn't looking forward to doing this pranayama for forty-five minutes either. But like a lot of things in life, once you get started it is easier than you think.

I stood naked in the early morning hour right out of bed, just to give you a visual, in an Agnisara position on my bright orange yoga mat stained by dirty hands and feet. The position to me is known as a horse stance from my time in martial arts. My feet were parallel, double shoulder distance apart, knees bent and gently pressed out away from each other. I slightly leaned forward bent at the hip with a straight elongated back and spine that extended on up my neck into the skull of my head, with my hands resting lightly on my knees, arms relaxed, but straight.

Similar to Kapalabhati I exhaled through my nose squeezing my stomach towards my spine and relaxing it for the inhale. I slowly started to detail the exhale beginning with the low belly. I pulled it in towards my spine from the pubic bone working the sensation and abdomen all the way up under the rib cage. My eyes witnessed the unusual but conscious contraction of my low and mid torso. After several exhales I held my breath out until I was slightly uncomfortable then released it for a natural inhale followed by a few unguided but conscious natural breaths.

Relaxing in between several non-traditional rounds of Agnisara I would stand straight up in Tadasana, feet one shoulder width apart for a breath or two giving my legs and back a rest. I also stretched into a back bend and forward fold before starting again as my body felt naturally called to do. There was an amazing amount of mucus discharge and I blew my nose and spit several times while thinking my desire for cheese, chocolate and other starching foods may not be in my body's best interest.

As I continued to deepen my experience with Agnisara, I included Mula bandha contracting my pelvic floor, Uddiana bandha contracting my belly as described, and Jalahara bandha bending my head forward contracting the throat and stretching the back of my neck.

While holding my breath out, I started rolling my abdomen further back, up and under my rib cage. I would not inhale as I released and contracted my belly in a fluid circular motion. This is where it started getting interesting.

I was about thirty minutes into this pranayama when I, my body, my spirit, my energetic emotional self spontaneously started exhaling forcefully with the emotions of anger, frustration and disappointment, dis-charging connections to my past triggered by my nudity, my genitalia, my penis dangling in between my legs. Breathing into and through the emotion of past lovers and desperate choices, I turned the experience and power of this pranayama into a healing of forgiveness and passion to make better choices for my body, mind and soul.

I deliberately began forgiving myself, my emotional physical self for not going deeper into the feeling of loneliness, separation and anxiety sooner than this present moment. I breathed tearfully determined to understand, heal, integrate and release what was not serving me for my highest good once and for all.

I felt a deep connection to something wiser than the self I knew before I started this pranayama. It was another part of my being that patiently waited for an opportunity to introduce itself to me once again and remind me that I am loved more than this little ego will ever understand from its separated point of view.

The feeling I was immersed in was unconditional love. Part of the frustration I felt was why do I keep forgetting this connection? It is always just a breath away being connected to... to... something beyond a description of mere, easily distorted words. Love and the many levels of it are hard to convey to its truest depth, but worth a try. I love a sandwich. I love my car. I love my dog. I love my children. I love my partner. I love my soulmate. I love myself. I love love.

Can you feel the difference and depth between each of the above statements? It is very hard for me to put in words what I felt and how it felt as it permeated my whole being. Heart opening, bursting energy broadcasting out of the pours of my skin, flushed with electric tingles throughout my body silencing my mind to feelings and presence. I was *being in love*. Warm tears of gratitude flowed down my face as I ever so slowly returned to solidity of the floor under my bare feet in my room in the back of my house alone but OK.

Kundalini

Dormant Power to Enlightenment

There are many views, myths and fears when it comes to kundalini. I look at the word "Kundalini" as both an adjective and a noun. The adjective Kundalini describes a particular style of yoga that prepares you for the experience and integration of the noun Kundalini into your body, mind and life. The yoga is not Kundalini. The noun Kundalini is real, but resides dormant deep within your body's first chakra. It is the true desire to know oneself by balancing the chakra system that I believe, awakens this force of enlightened energy. Once the balance (ideally) of the first six chakras has occurred (or not) the Kundalini may rise (or not) through the Sushumna to the third eye and crown chakras, initiating one with a deeper perspective and understanding of life.

Here are some questions to ask yourself if you are interested in awakening Kundalini:

- Am I ready to surrender my view of life as I know it now?
- Am I ready to let go of who and what I think I am?
- Am I ready to be of service?

From the movie 'Awaken' about Yogananda's life, here's a quote: "Find your spine."

The following two paragraphs are from my research online that I happen to agree with:

Kundalini can be understood in scientific, medically acceptable terms simply "by working forwards from the state of disease and imbalance to the state of optimal healthy function, for example, from ulcerative colitis to perfect digestive health. Proper digestive power is a manifestation of kundalini awakening in manipura chakra (3rd), just as clear vision, both external and intuitive, is a sign of ajna chakra's awakening (6th). Kundalini awakened takes us beyond just optimal health but to the state of human perfection, our full potential.

Full awakening of Kundalini is the elusive state of perfect physical and mental health which by normal standards is impossible to achieve but by stepping out of the cultural box quite possible. This is the state of some great yogis. Perhaps doctors and scientists should take to these practices, under proper guidance, and try to understand and interpret their experiences in the light of the yogic scriptural descriptions. In this way yogic and medical psychophysiology will surely converge - for the two are experiencing and analyzing the same single subject - the human body, mind and heart.

By Dr. Karl Nespor, Czechoslovakia Bihar School of Yoga and Bihar Yoga Bharati.

And now

Breathwork

An Umbrella word for
Different Conscious Breathing Exercises
and

my
Thirteen Breaths to Freedom
Sequence

www.James-Beard.com

Breathwork

Breath = Life

Work = Effort

Breathwork Defined

Below I have included four definitions: mine, the International Breathwork Foundation's (IBF) and the last from a well-known Breathworker whom I have never met in person but I have enjoyed some interactions with her via the internet.

1. Breathwork is a phenomenal mind altering, aerobic, conscious, breathing exercise designed to help you understand and heal yourself physically, mentally, emotionally, energetically, and spiritually.

IBF (International Breathwork Foundation) definitions accepted by the United Nations:

2. Conscious breathing is the practice of breathing with awareness, intention and attention to inner experience, in the present moment.

3. Breathwork is a dynamic body-mind practice using conscious breathing techniques for enhanced health, wellbeing and personal transformation.

One of the original founders of the IBF Gunnell Minett's definition:

4. Breathwork is the intentional alteration of the breathing pattern for healing and mind-expanding purposes.

As you can see they are very similar. They point in a comparable direction but really don't give a complete feeling of what Breathwork is, that is until one has experienced Breathwork. Then the definitions make more sense because your experience has filled in the blank space of "what" and "why" as you understand inner experience and personal transformation.

Breathwork Styles

Breathwork

Rebirthing	Pranayama	Qigong
Leonard Orr		
Integravtive Rebirthing	Holotropic Breathwork	Coherent Breathing
Vivation Jim Leonard	Stan Grof	Stephen Elliot
Liberation Breathing		5 per min 2004
Sondra Ray	Shamanic Breathwork	
Radiance Breathwork		Richard Brown &
Gay Hendrix	Holographic Breathing	Patricia Gerbarg
Integravtive Breathing	Martin Jones	
Clarity Breathwork		Art of Living
Therapeutic Breathwork	Breath of Life	Contemporary
	8 key breaths	
Transformational Breath		Breathology
Conscious Connected	MCO	
Breathing		Zen Breathwork
	Biodynamic Breathwork	
and others	Buteyko	Tummo	Maneuvers
	1950, 1968, 1980	WHM	Toynbee & Valsalva
	Asthma		

Western origins of Breathwork, their founders and a clue.

Rebirthing	Leonard Orr	4 short 1 long
Transformational	Judith Kravitz	Relax the jaw, find your belly
Holotropic	Stan Grof	Music-driven, Chakra-influenced
Holographic	Martin Jones	Chewing gum
Coherent Breathing	Stephen Elliot	6 in - 6 out
Buteyko	Dr. Buteyko	Asthma
Conscious Connected Breathing		No pause, seamless
Radiance Breathwork	Gay Hendrix	Rock the hips, 3 yes's - 3 no's

Maneuvers — Two Western medical practices involving the breath

Toynbee	Dr. Toynbee	Nose and ears
Valsalva	Dr. Valsalva	Belly push to reset the vagus nerve

Contemporary Breathing & birthing

Lamaze — He he ha ha

Bradley Method — Why natural childbirth? The kind of pregnancy, labor, and birth our children experience has a profound and lifelong effect on their health, including their mental, emotional, and physical health. The Bradley Method® attempts to give babies the best possible start in life by teaching soon to be parents how to have a natural pregnancy and natural childbirth.

In the world of Breathwork I know here in the West, here are some standards.

Sitter and breather	Writing
One to three hour session, (10 recommended)	Drawing
Group breathings	Movement
Group process	Music

Possible Breathwork Benefits

The following is a list of common possible benefits of conscious breathing I discovered from my years in the Breathwork field. They are listed here not to be redundant in the following Breathwork styles and practices.

- 70% toxin removal (metabolic waste) with proper efficient breathing
- Stress reduction
- Emotional healing, revelation and discharge
- Empowerment
- Heightened senses
- Spiritual understanding and connection
- Freedom
- Inner gifts revealed (awakening or awakened)
- Change
- Forgiveness
- Unconditional love

Contradictory or unnerving

I am listing the following as contradictory but I truly believe if you are ready to face the self, yourself that you have created, consciously and subconsciously these are a beneficial part of Breathwork. Some say, deconstruction before reconstruction. I say, better out than in.

- Tetany or tetney
- Nausea
- Dizziness
- Vertigo
- Headache
- Tinnitus
- Facing your buried emotional self

Concerns

I highly recommend reading the book "The Ethics of Caring" by Kylea Taylor if you are a Breathworker or planning on taking some Breathwork sessions. It covers a lot of material and is Breathwork-based. The part about 'transference and counter-transference' stood out for me, the subtle energy exchange between client and practitioner. I also recommend recognizing the difference between "Drama and Discharge" and time for integration, introspection and reflection.

"The Ethics of Caring" by Kylea Taylor is written for psychotherapists, bodyworkers, medical practitioners, clergy and spiritual teachers, hypnotherapists, acupuncturists, chiropractors, medical support personnel, and teachers who want to become more conscious in their relationships with clients. Kylea Taylor sees ethics as the practice of moving toward wholeness as human beings, rather than feeling constricted by the imposition of external rules. The Ethics of Caring provides a new model with some tools for navigating the deep and often confusing relationship between client and caregiver and for preventing the harmful consequences of ethical misconduct.

Powerful, shared experiences in the context of the therapeutic relationship can bring to the surface compelling fears, needs, and longings in both the client and the caregiver. There are many therapeutic moments of consciousness expansion during traditional therapy; for example, when a client's belief system suddenly changes, or when there is a deepening of intimacy and spiritual connection within the therapeutic relationship. The use of current methods such as hypnosis, breathwork, meditation, massage, EMDR, acupuncture, and shamanic techniques can increase the likelihood of profound and intense client/caregiver interactions. These may bring surprisingly subtle and powerful challenges to caregivers. Therapists, ministers, and other caregivers often feel that they will have no difficulty maintaining ethical conduct. Yet, the non-ordinary states of consciousness occurring in these profound therapeutic moments can change easily avoidable pitfalls into invisible, deep quagmires.

In ethical helping relationships, caregivers support their clients, but are careful not to let their own fears, desires, or spiritual longings distort their clients' process. Only by understanding their own vulnerabilities and by deeply considering the ways in which these affect their interactions with others, can caregivers hope to enter more fully into truly healing relationships with their clients."

Excerpt from Kylea Taylor's website Thank you Kylea.

There are many ways to use and apply Breathwork in your life. They range from general well-being to insightfully spiritual. There are several keys to use. Here are a few:

- Ask a good question?
- Create a powerful affirmation.
- Surrender to the power within.
- Persevere.
- Daily practice, did I write daily practice? Do I need to write it again?

Remember to trust yourself, if one Breathworker doesn't feel good, try another.

The journey continues

Rebirthing Breathwork

Leonard Orr is the founder of Rebirthing. I have read and heard several stories of how Rebirthing originated, from he started in his bathtub to he was taught in India by a man named Babaji. Leonard wrote a book titled; 'The Story of Rebirthing' easily found on line, a recommended read for Breathworkers of all types.

Rebirthers believe in cerebral memory, cellular memory and the mind which is distributed throughout the body. And more recent studies from the book Brain Maker the author writes about the intelligence of the gut to validate this belief further and the influence of your birth process has on the rest of your physical life.

Rebirthing Breathwork practitioners believe that the perception and interpretation of one's birth albeit subconscious, has a deep effect on one's psyche and shapes one's ideals and experience of life, self, and the world in ways of which one is mostly unaware.

Leonard believes deeply in being immortal and that it is a matter of changing our internal beliefs that we have learned throughout our life to overcome our mortality. He believes these beliefs are inherent, traditional, and learned from the example of our parents, family, education and culture.

My Experience

Today I was in a debate with the lazy part of myself again. Because I just want to finish this book. I was debating whether or not I would dedicate a fresh new forty-five minutes to Rebirthing. And it is right here that I will confess my love for Breathwork one more time. I love Breathwork and the magical mystical revelations that come from a devoted practice. Once again I am in awe of where I went with the energy of the breath this morning.

January 17th, 2017, I woke up just before 5 am and started a self-led rebirthing session. I have been teaching and guiding myself since the 80's long before I knew I was going to be teaching Breathwork and Life 101, if you will. For a long time I thought I was destined to be an electrician/technician for the rest of my working career. But like the line in the movie, 'A Knight's Tale' William's dad told him, "Change your stars boy, change your stars." I have done that for myself and I give great credit to Breathwork because of its revealing and empowering abilities and so much more.

I wasn't expecting much this morning from a forty-five minute session but the insights started unfolding around twenty minutes into the Rebirthing session. I got out of bed and found a pencil and paper to catch the following. My body was relaxed, all but what I thought it took to breathe until I started to mentally and sensationally explore my diaphragm and let go of my abdominal muscles. I focused on my diaphragm, where it attached, the weight of my stomach and liver and then my breathing changed and became more heart centered. I started getting the impression of a baby breathing feeling my rib cage flex with each breath. My spine started to pop with each deep diaphragmatic exhale. I continued to explore the sensation of my diaphragm, from my sternum to my floating ribs along the perimeter of my rib cage and the attachment to my spine. I naturally held my breath out really feeling the pull of the diaphragm with relaxed abs. (They were not pushing in.)

Next I was in an altered state looking into my mother's eyes suckling on her breast not breathing but feeling the sensation of swallowing her milk and the unspoken communication between us. I was taking it all in, in that pause of a breath looking deep into the love in her eyes, the communication between our bodies, her breast and my mouth, our scents and our energetic connection, so much information happening at once. We were each other's creator. She was creating me as a child and I was creating her as a mother, my mother, I, her child on so many levels it is hard to put into words. We were one and it was timeless. The exchange in energy, from chemical inputs, our bonding presence and vibrant stillness in the connection between mother, child and God, the recognition of we, in the soul gaze of breastfeeding was way beyond the mere words I am typing here.

On a logical mental note my present fifty-four year old altered mind was floating around this revelation like the moon does the earth. I recalled a talk I heard on the radio about a new discovery about breastfeeding. The nipple not only produces milk, nutrients and endorphins it also has receptors that take in the baby's saliva for information on the baby's needs for optimum health. It is an exchange between mother and baby on profound levels. And that thought lead me to lovers kissing and loving each other and if there was an exchange at this level too, way beyond the physical into the spiritual realm and everything in between. The answer I received was, 'of course' and I continued to spiral around this informational vortex in deep gratitude murmuring, "Thank you, Thank you, Thank you. The feelings and insights were overwhelming and seemed a lot longer than fifty-five minutes of breathing.

As I came back to this reality in my altered state of mind, I thought why would someone change the name of Rebirthing? Is there really any need to change it? The word "Rebirthing" says it all and poses a trigger to help you remember your perfection before birth.

As I solidified back into my everyday human form I recalled my days of teaching "The Sacred Breath" at Body Mind Expos and the recognition of self-discovery I was trying to claim as my own.

After a failed attempt at marketing and recognition that very few people had heard of Breathwork, I found part of my purpose was to offer "An Introduction to Breathwork". So I pulled my ego, to the best of my ability, out of the equation and began to offer Breathwork with no agenda or any need to make a name for myself. In my reality I do believe the world; your world and my world can be uplifted if more people had Breathwork or conscious breathing in their life. It is a service offered around the world under many names and by a variety of practitioners, if it is received wonderful, if it is not wonder full.

In my world I recognized that it is not me doing the work for others. It is the spirit, the soul, the God spark, Christ consciousness, and breath, the life force that sustains the life we all live here on earth. In my reality I only wish you the peace and love I have found for myself doing Breathwork. I didn't find it in religion, shamanism, crystals, or western yoga. Breathwork found me at a party and I said yes. What I was looking for was inside of me the whole time, connected to the present moment with the simple act of conscious breathing.

♥ ♥

There are hundreds if not thousands of Breathwork Practitioners that teach and practice Rebirthing. Many of them have coined a name of their own that were influenced by Rebirthing but stepped away from their roots with a variation they felt called to do.

The following are some of the names I am aware of at this time that still exist:

Radiance Breathwork	Integrative Breathwork	Vivation
Therapeutic Breathwork	Clarity Breathwork	
Alchemy of Breath	Including Transformational Breathwork	
Breath Mastery	Many others have faded away.	

If you noticed I didn't write a "**How to:**" bullet point for rebirthing. I am not a certified rebirther just experienced. May I suggest you find a Rebirther or....

Here's another suggestion: Breathe full consciously connected breaths for forty-five minutes. Practice daily, witness and journal.

What was your experience?

Did you stay connected with your breath? If not, you now have part of an understanding of the role of a sitter.

What worked for you? (set and setting)

What was your hope? (hidden agenda)

Did you have expectations?

Did you have an intention or leave it open for the highest good?

Did you feel resistance or an urgency to stop? (keep breathing)

Was it worth your time and effort?

Are you willing to start a daily practice?

Transformational

You may see the word transformational with breathing or Breathwork following it or the word transformations by itself if you search it on line. Today I am exploring **Transformational Breath®** that was created by Judith Kravitz. I like that she healed herself of throat cancer with the use of Breathwork in 1979. I understand she received Rebirthing sessions with Leonard Orr and Breathwork complemented her training in the holistic and metaphysical arts which in turn took her healing to another level and that developed into Transformational Breath®. It written she has trained over a hundred thousand people around the world in the practice Transformational Breath®. It has four levels and a professional level. It is quite the business model.

For me I found this practice to be one of the more enthusiastic conscious breathing practices in the Breathwork field that I am aware of. It was like the practitioner wanted me to have an experience. They have tools to help you breathe freely and deeply complete body charts with points of interest and meaning. They use sound, as in toning, singing or yelling to help you release suppressed emotions and they use movement. They are intent that you relax your jaw while you breathe fully in and out of your mouth and much more.

My Experience

On January 18th, 2017, I woke up with a slight headache thinking and feeling I don't want to do anything but lie in bed. A gentle voice spoke up from behind the lazy painful feeling trying to persuade me to cancel today's appointments and said, "Start breathing the Transformational way." I heard it at 6:30 and laid there for another ten minutes witnessing the different pieces of myself arguing before I got out of bed to do 100 breaths, arms up inhale, pull down exhale with one knee coming up and alternating knees with each breath similar to Bhastrika. I lost count several times so I made sure I did over a hundred breaths marching around my bedroom in red pajama bottoms and my old business long sleeve tee shirt with 'Stretch Yourself' written on the sleeves and my spectrum spiral on my chest.

I was breathing heavy with tired arms and legs with another part of me wondering what the heck I was doing up so early in the morning. I sat at the top of my bed and continued breathing with an open mouth, relaxed jaw and full complete heart-centered breaths. I started recalling all of the transformational techniques and tricks. I grabbed the mouthpiece that I use for my Intro to Breathwork talks and briefly thought of where it had been. I looked at it while breathing and finally wiped it on my sleeve with a shoulder shrug and popped it in my mouth being a true guinea pig.

Memories of previous Transformational Breath™ sessions flooded in. Like the evening I first met Judith at the first Breathwork Immersion when I received this mouth piece. I had purposely kept my mouth close-lipped hoping to receive one and now it was in my mouth again. It changed the natural flow of breath into my mouth this morning and an unexpected column of air hit the back of my throat. The mouth piece is hard, bulky plastic that I jokingly call a "turbo" during my talks because it increases the volume of air. It takes a little getting use too. But this morning my body was rejecting it with gag reflexes.

I kept the plastic surgical mouth piece in my mouth for ten minutes, continuing to breathe in a seated position in my bed. I took it out of my mouth with one last gag. I continued breathing full and fast, at the pace the 100 breaths created before I naturally went into a suspended breath tingling from head to toe. I slid out of my bed on to my hardwood floor to breathe flat on my back while shaking my limbs, pounding my fists on the floor and rocking my head back and forth. I didn't make any sounds, tones or screams because I thought my roommate had to already be wondering what I was doing. I continued breathing and slipped back into another suspended breath of insight and ecstasy.

A beautiful friend of mine knocked on my front door to pick up a package so early in the morning. I just kept breathing as I answered without a word. She just looked me, smiling, puzzled and asked, "What are you on? I kept breathing as I loaded her car, received a hug from her and finally whispered in her ear "Transformational Breathing day." She knew I was writing this book.

The Transformational Breath® gets me high and energized at first but as I continue past that feeling, I become deeply connected to something I consider spiritual, a connection that comes from sensations, memories, knowing, intuition, healing and satisfaction. Oh! By the way, the headache is gone, forgot all about it until proofreading the next day.

~~~~~~

I am also not certified in Transformational Breath® but I am experienced and love it. There are plenty of clues in my experience for you to try. Remember forty-five minutes at least is the time to devote to it. Allow time for integration. Be the witness and trust the truest part of yourself.

I highly recommend finding a Breathworker near for your first few Breathwork experiences.

Holotropic Breathwork™

Holo = Whole

Tropic = Moving towards

Moving towards wholeness

Stan Grof is a pioneer in the states of consciousness and non-ordinary states of consciousness.

Holotropic is a practice that uses breathing and other elements to allow access to non-ordinary states for the purpose of self-exploration and self-discovery.

It is a very well-known Breathwork practice that has made its way around the world over the last forty years. Stan Grof is still very active in it at 85 years old. I have met him a couple of times over the years and listened to his talks that can easily be found with a Google search. One of my favorites is "Spiritual Emergencies: Understanding and Treatment of Psychospiritual Crisis." The following is an excerpt:

> One of the most important implications of the research of Holotropic states is the realization that many of the conditions, which are currently diagnosed as psychotic and indiscriminately treated by suppressive medication, are actually difficult stages of a radical personality transformation and of spiritual opening. If they are correctly understood and supported, these psychospiritual crises can result in emotional and psychosomatic healing, remarkable psychological transformation, and consciousness evolution (Grof and Grof 1989, 1990).

The Holotropic method comprises five elements including a sitter and breather:

1. Group sharing
2. Intensified breathing
3. Evocative music
4. Focused body work
5. Expressive drawing (mandalas)

Holotropic Breathwork™ has several components with very little variety that comes from the facilitator.

- A safe container (set and setting) where you will be in a secure area between one and three hours for a full session.
- An HB facilitator may ask you to increase your breathing or simply bring your awareness to your breath. (I have experienced both.)
- Music with no words.
- Closure (making sure you are good to go back out into the world)

To have a true experience of Holotropic Breathwork™ go to their website www.holotropic.com and you will find an event under lectures and workshops.

I am not a certified HB practitioner but I am experienced in Holotropic Breathwork™. I checked online to see if there was a workshop in my area to write from a new experience of HB but found none near me. Below I share two past experiences with HB where Stan Grof was present. My apologies for the incongruity in this writing but to be true to the work this is how this will be. Holotropic Breathwork™ has played a big role in the world of Breathwork and I do not want to do it injustice. And now I smile, because here is part of my past experience with HB.

My Experience

I believe the year was 2003 when an acquaintance of mine named Lee asked if I would like to go with him to a weekend Holotropic Breathwork™ workshop. "Of course," I said, he knew I was teaching Breathwork. It was advertised. "Meet the Grandfather of Breathwork, Stan Grof Before He Retires." When the time came to go Lee backed out. Once again I was leaving on an adventure by myself. I was excited, a full weekend of Breathwork and I am not facilitating. This was my time to Breathe and I went with great expectations.

The HB workshop was in the Washington DC area a half day drive from Raleigh, NC. It started Friday night with an introductory talk by Stan Grof. I listened and wondered when we were going to breathe. Stan just talked. I was disappointed. No Breathwork the first night. What?

Saturday morning those that signed up for the whole weekend gathered to be paired up as sitters and breathers. At that time I had long hair down my back and a beard. The lady I had met the night before only went for the Friday night talk. I was so hoping she would change her mind as she left me with the words, "I will sleep on it." So I looked around to catch the eye of someone else looking for a partner. Many eyes quickly looked away until there were just two us of standing there, myself and another lady dressed in black. I smiled as I felt her reluctance and gently approached her. Being the last kid picked was nothing new to me, she looked shocked.

We were informed of what to do with our roles as breather and sitter and I offered her the choice to breathe or sit first. She chose breathe. I asked what she needed from me as a sitter/supporter and she told me, nothing. The music started and the breathers were told to breathe and that was it. There were no directions other than that. My partner went into a kundalini yoga breathing posture doing Agnisara. Stan walked by watched her for a curious moment, looked at me with a smile and the slightest of a shoulder shrug before moving on. I sat and watched ready with tissue and water. The music peaked and faded. Then I walked her to another room for her to draw a mandala. We broke for lunch and then it was my turn.

I asked my sitter to do one thing for me. It was really simple. I asked her to smile at me when I opened my eyes. That was it. Whoever the DJ was playing for the second session rocked the house, at least mine. (I wish I would have received his play list as part of the event.) I was moved. I started breathing slowly recognizing I was free to do what I thought was best for me. I started off deliberate, detailed and progressively built up the pace of my conscious connected breaths to a holding of the inhale. My body relaxed, my mind cleared and my energy expanded. The music was invigorating and continued building with a great beat. After another holding of my breath I opened my eyes to ground myself. My sitter looked at me with a dropped jaw and question marked pupils of surprise. I was vibrating at a higher frequency. I was electric and couldn't take the music anymore lying down. I needed to dance, move and flow.

I found an open spot on the floor with enough room to bounce jump spin crawl and breathe. I was an animal, instinctually evolving through the movement. The assistants quickly arrived to block the door near me with their arms spread out like Mother Mary. I was trance dancing with no intention to go anywhere. But they stayed put in their low vibe. I felt and perceived fear and control coming from them. Their intention was good but I was hoping for love. I trusted the movements my body chose, keeping the connection to energetic flow with my mind as a silent witness. The animal in me shied away from the overly concerned assistants, slowing my dance to a pace of a captive animal. I let the breath go or the music changed and I stopped, looking at the guards of the door with a little head shake back and forth, before returning to my spot on the floor to breathe. I smiled at my dumbfounded sitter who never left her spot before I closed my eyes.

The music eventually slowed to a classical pace my mom would listen to and I decided it was time for my mandala. Not my best art but a right brain understanding and memory of my HB experience.

Stan came by to ask how I was. I mumbled something about Shakti in my altered state and shook my head. We broke for an uneventful dinner and returned for a group sharing. Divided into small groups we headed off to smaller break out rooms to share our experience. The lady holding space for our group was very sweet and one of the human wall surrounding me as I went through my cathartic trance dance. After we shared what we were willing to share from one person saying, "I don't get it. Nothing happened." to me, a lot happened and I was still trying to understand it. I went through an internal evolution from the floor to crawling, bent in a Neanderthal position to standing to falling down and repeating until I couldn't take the weight of the fear surrounding me. Even though I knew they meant well.

After we closed our session I asked the lady facilitating our group what the next day entailed. She said it would be more sharing and Stan talking. I asked her if she thought it would help me with an understanding of my experience. She didn't need to say anything her facial expression and body language was enough. My little ego left that night with two thoughts.

1. One Breathwork session, I get paid to sit and now I am paying to do it.
2. If Stan Grof is the Grandfather of Breathwork (as the workshop was advertised) then I am the Grandson of Breathwork.

I was at another event Stan Grof was facilitating. My sitter was so good this time that she swatted away Ann Harrison a former president of the Australian Association for Professional Rebirthers that tried to sit down next to me and assist with my session. I had told my sitter not to let anyone near me except her. She also smiled, as asked, and pulled on my neck to relief some tension when I requested it. It was a wonderful session for both of us. After the closure of the session I politely waited by a door to let someone in the room, that gesture put me next to Stan. When he turned to see who was standing beside him, he looked into my eyes with childlike wonder emitting from his 80 year body and face as he spoke the words, "Look at all the light in your eyes."

"Breathwork," I said with a smile, "Breathwork."

Holographic Breathing

Holographic Breathing came to Martin Jones whilst he was dying of Lymes Disease. He felt that he was losing the battle, and to see what it was, one day whilst watching his breath, he let the disease take him. He likened the experience to going through the folds of death, until coming to the other side, and a light. On coming back from that journey Holographic Breathing started by its self, it just began, and became his natural breath. Happily over a period of time this Breathing helped him recover from the Lymes Disease.

In Holographic Breathing - the lips are closed, the tongue is on the roof of the mouth, and then there is a small, relaxed small motion of the jaw - on the in breath the jaw gently opens and on the out breath the jaw gently closes.

When Learning Holographic Breathing in a correct way this movement synchronizes with the same movement that is within us as cellular memory. As this cellular memory awakens there is a sense of deep relaxation and moving into our selves.

To learn Holographic Breathing and to have that experience, it is best to view the Free Video Tutorials. These provide a very relaxed way of moving the mouth with the breath and letting that activation naturally happen. From there, there is an integrated journey that takes this experience through the whole body and energies. You can view these videos at www.holographic-breathing.com or Face book Group Free Learn Holographic Breathing.

I came across Martin Jones' Holographic Breathing on line while doing some research for a talk I giving to the America Hypnosis Association. At first I thought it was just another person doing an off shoot from Holotropic Breathwork like what has happened with Rebirthing and myself. But I was quite pleased I got past my history, judgement and personal wound, because his story is so powerful. It lets us all know what we are capable of if we can just slow down and breathe. We can heal and understand the depths of what it is to be human. I am glad I opened his website www.holographic-breathing.com and listened to his story. I share it in all my 'Introduction to Breathwork' talks.

My Experience

On January 19th, 2017, I did my second self-led breath session devoted to Holographic Breathing this time. First I needed to clear my mind of more ideas for promoting this material before I finally settled into a rhythmic breath of simulating chewing gum. My body relaxed, the afternoon sounds faded to the background and I focused on my maxilla and breathed. Before I knew it my body was snoring, mouth open and I was sporadically dreaming. I would catch myself drifting back and forth across the fine line of consciousness and subconscious mental wandering with my mouth hanging open with a heavy breath.

Sometimes the snore would make me aware and sometimes the tickle of my lips slowly peeling apart would bring me back to consciously moving my jaw in rhythm of my breath. At one point I was looking at the flowers and shrubs in my back yard before I realized I was still lying in my bed with my eye mask on. I was looking through it as my focus drifted away from my maxilla in an altered state to my backyard.

I felt a wonderful pulse moving my whole body coming from my diaphragm. It is hard to describe in words. As I witnessed it, I was wondering if this is what Stephen Elliot referred to as the "Valsalva Wave." It was like a feeling I got from a Chi machine I tried at a Body Mind Expo where I rested the lower part of my calves just above my ankles on it while lying on my back. Then it swung my legs back and forth parallel to the floor creating an interesting ripple or harmonic wave up through my body.

My roommate came home about a half hour into this breathing session. I took note of the energy shift in my awareness or I could say my house. I continued breathing with focus on the task at hand. I felt and noticed a presence of beings, or I could say people interacting with me on another level. It was surreal. Then they all left at the same time, walking away to my surprise up some steps, off to my left side. Then I was back in bed my breathing with a realization this session was over. I looked at the time and smiled I had three minutes to go for a full forty-five-minute session.

~~~~~~

What is your purpose for breathing? Why?

What is your intention? State it and let it go.

Breathe in. Breathe out. Repeat.

Learn, release, empower.

Coherent Breathing

There is a lot to Stephen Elliot but my focus is his Coherent Breathing method. He holds multiple patents, copyrights and trademarks on methods and systems supporting Coherent Breathing amongst many other scientifically backed theories.

He is the modern day re-discoverer of the respiratory arterial pressure wave and has patents issued and pending on its measurement and as a basis of biofeedback. Stephen with Dr. Bob Grove coined the name "Valsalva Wave" describing the wholistic arterial and venous wave phenomenon that occurs in the circulatory system when relaxing and breathing coherently.

Stephen has contributed substantially to the contemporary understanding of the heart rate variability phenomenon and its physiology.

He is the inventor of the Six Bridges method which combines Coherent Breathing with conscious relaxation of certain anatomical zones called "bridges." For more information about Stephen and his passion and patents, check out his website coherentbreathing.org or coherence.com

I heard about Coherent Breathing at the Breathwork Immersion 2013 from Richard Brown and Patricia Gerbarg's Power Point talk and shared exercises. I was quite impressed in what they have done around the world and the research in the science community. You may want to check them out too.

Steve is a down to earth pioneer in the understanding of himself and the human design.

My Experience

The morning of January 19th, 2017, I had intended to do Coherent Breathing. What I demonstrate and teach as a six in, six out breath count. I started at 7:13 thinking I would finish at 8:00. Have I mentioned I love Breathwork?

I started breathing and counting and thinking I need to make or just buy Stephen's CD. One bell for inhale and one bell for exhale every six seconds because counting kept me in my mind. I checked the time at 7:26, thirteen minutes into Coherent Breathing. I felt good and relaxed and had a good feel or sense of the six second timing by the rhythm and resistance of my body. So I started to breathe with feeling taking me deeper into my body. Insights and ideas for this book and workshop started to flow into my mind and awareness with a really good feeling about it, complete with images.

I noticed I would stop consciously breathing at the end of the exhale and in that pause I would feel my body deepen the relaxation, borderline of falling asleep or a precursor for an Out of Body Experience. It felt very similar to the depth of body awareness I had back when I was eighteen and had my first out-of-body-experience. Now my body is fifty-four and comes with a few aches and pains. I was able to move and spread out the vibration I was feeling in my legs and arms into my torso region and face. My mind was consciously aware of my body lightly snoring as I continued to move the vibrant energy into and through the pain and stiffness in my hips and buttocks with my mind. This allowed my body not to ground and distract me from going deeper as I felt the sensations of floating starting to occur.

It only felt like minutes had passed and I didn't want to check the time and disturb the vibrant healing energy humming all throughout my body. I love this place, space and frequency of being or deep meditation.

I was walking down a white marble patio with a low thick ornate railing and tall carved columns supporting the floor above. I was enjoying the view of the harbor before me with a couple of well-defined cruise ships anchored offshore with some random yachts anchored near them on this beautiful day when I realized I was also back in my bed breathing. The wobble in my mind brought me back to my bed and breathing body with a warm feeling of the Caribbean in tow, a complete contrast to the grey drizzle outside my window.

I continued breathing, feeling and exploring in awe until I could no longer ignore the persistent hunger pain coming from my stomach under my left ribs. I looked at the time thinking it's got to be close to forty-five minutes and was quite surprised to see the time read 8:38. What a way to start my day.

~~~~~~

I am not certified in this one either but I have an understanding and experience.

Try this:

1. Seamlessly breathe in for six seconds and breathe out for six seconds.
2. Devote a good amount of time to it.
3. Record how you felt before and after Coherent Breathing.
4. Daily Practice
5. Daily Practice
6. Consistent Daily Practice.....

Buteyko Breathing

If you are a Breathworker or highly interested in the power of your breath, Buteyko Breathing is worth taking a look at. It is known as an alternative treatment for asthma. Dr. Buteyko was born outside of Kiev, Ukraine in 1923 and passed in 2003. His life story can easily be found with a quick search on the web. What caught my interest was the success he had in healing asthma and how his lab was shut down afterward. This is one of the human conditions, the control of information. With that in mind there is a lot written on Dr. Buteyko's work and even I will add a twist to it.

The truth be told, when we slow down, sit or lie, unplug and focus on our breath, miracles can happen. The problem with today's pace is, that it is so simple, it sounds too good to be true. The value or simple acceptance, we have put into being entertained, pleased and distracted from taking a good look at ourselves and the world around us by the quick fix marketing gimmicks has taken a toll on our health and wellbeing. Buteyko Breathing is one more Breathwork tool to add to an alternative holistic way of life.

I wish you the best in sorting through the information highway and by now you know what I really wish for you is a steady daily practice of a breathwork style all your own.

My Experience

This morning I started doing what I could recall of Buteyko breathing. I came across some audio cassette tapes in a truck stop in 1998 titled "Breathe Easy" that referred to this type of breathing. The idea was to work up to holding your breath out comfortably for forty-five seconds. I listened and practiced while driving back then. I do not recommend doing any of these exercises while driving, long story short I ended up in a country ditch next to the road thinking I would make to the church parking lot to finish my breathing exercise. Anyway I listened, breathed and practiced. I didn't have asthma but I did have a thirst for anything about breathing and its benefits.

I did a little research online and found nothing about the cassettes I listened to so long ago. But I did find the world has started to recognize the importance of breathing. There was something about isometrics and breath counts and this is what I did on this day of the President Trump's inauguration. Something people around the world could have benefitted from, instead of watching the news.

I did a couple rounds of Conscious Breathing and then held my breath out and counted to 21 before I felt the mammalian reflex to breathe, the uncomfortable pull on my diaphragm. My understanding was to divide the hold time by 3. Then I did a minute of natural but Conscious Breathing and held my breath out for 7 seconds, the divided time. I repeated this pattern a couple of times before holding my breath out for 33 seconds an increase of 11 seconds. This is what you want to accomplish, an increase in easy retention. So if you held your breath out easily for 12 seconds then your rounds would be 4 second retentions: One third the time of the long hold time to train your body.

After another few rounds of seven seconds holds I held my breath out for over forty-five seconds meeting the ideal of the practice. I breathed some nice full rounds of conscious breathing and slipped into a suspended breath state of altered consciousness that felt really nice. I reflected over the years and some of the Breathwork experiences I had been through.

One was of a lady that offered a Buteyko breakout session at the Breathwork Immersion at the Omega Institute 2013. She talked about the science and gas exchange of the breath and how she had asthma herself. I asked her if she had heard that asthma is an emotional body symptom of un-cried tears. I had heard this in my herbalist class so I shared it with her. She didn't agree but came up to me later in the week-long conference and told me Stan Grof said the same thing to her. It was a wonderful validation for both of us.

I was also recalling how long I have been dedicated to this cause of helping people learn about alternative healing, Breathwork and spreading the word of this amazing magical healing practice that sounds too good to be true. "You were just breathing?!" I smile at such comments now and answer,

"Yes, just breathing."

!!!

I am definitely not certified in Buteyko, to much science for me. But I do believe in the practice and discipline, especially if you have asthma.

Check out Dr Buteyko's online videos or find a book. Or better yet read the above again and apply.

Breath hold time divided by three.

Tummo

Inner Fire Meditation

Tummo is a breathing exercise and meditation that comes from Tibet. There are several different variations of teaching online I discovered from my research. My recent experience with Tummo mostly comes from the influence of Wim Hof, aka The Ice Man. Before that I had read about Tibetan monks that could melt the snow around them and warm and dry a wet blanket on their back as part of an initiation or test of this type of practice. I was quite intrigued with the power of this practice and our human abilities when trained and applied.

When I first met Wim Hof at weekend workshop in Malibu, CA, he taught us his version of Tummo preparing us for our first ice bath. Now he uses own name to describe his practice called the "Wim Hof Method." And the last workshop I did with him I didn't notice Tummo being mentioned or a pranayama breath like Bhastrika. (Just breathe m*#@#rf*#@rs, an inside joke to the WHM breathers.)

There is alot online about Tummo and alot of subtle and not so subtle variations. So I suggest if you feel something with the word Tummo, do some research and the same for the Iceman, Wim Hof. He has a ten week online program to prepare you for ice bathing. Remember trust yourself, your true self.

My Experience

Saturday night only one person showed up for my breathing circle. I opened the session with the Eight Key Breaths of Life by Edwin John Dingle that are regularly practiced at the Institute of Mentalphysics in Joshua Tree, CA. They are also from Tibet. Since I only had to facilitate one person (a regular) I took advantage and dedicated my Breathwork practice to Tummo breathing. I breathed awareness down two channels along my spine to the Dantian or Hara area of my body. They are located just below the belly button and towards the spine. I imagined, visualized and sensed pulling up earth energy and pulling down sky energy to my Hara. I felt the energy starting to build up and mentally moved it up my back to my head. It has been written to build it up and then release it through the central channel. I didn't feel that but I did feel the warmth and mentally moved it up my spine to my Medulla oblongata and across to my third eye. I found this practice to be a peaceful and warm experience. I was surprised how quickly the time passed. It just flew by.

Another way I look at Tummo is: It is a forced inhale and relaxed exhale. The energy channels are subtle but powerful when realized in their full potential.

Have fun with it and don't forget to trust yourself.

You may have noticed my writing is quite different when I am in an altered state and tonight I am not, just happily tired and looking forward to sleeping. Good night.

Early in the morning I woke up with a headache I just couldn't shake and didn't think to do the hundred breaths, it was bad. The headache was at the back inside of my skull, the left side of my medulla oblongata. I meditated for forty five minutes focusing on it not being there. Then my mind went back to a time years ago when I was being trained in the Raphael Light Healing Order and I had a similar headache at the base of my skull. Back then I focused on it during one of our guided exercises. When it finally released like a cork from a bottle, I understood what inspired the Roman Catholic Cathedrals. I was standing in a church or space in my head with ornate painted ceilings and life-size pictures of saints framed on every wall. That was what was revealed to me when that headache released. It was a personal revelation moving through this block to a vast expansion of open majestic, spirit and saint filled space on the other side.

I was hoping to accomplish the same thing this morning but I finally got out of bed and did a head stand for a minute or so, nothing changed. Still hurting I drank a big glass of water and went jogging in the early morning grey drizzle. Then I took a long shower and finally after I ate breakfast, I felt relief. I don't take pain meds unless it is totally unbearable.

Part of me is whispering delete the above it doesn't shine a good light on your experience. Truth be told, that part of me is right and it is afraid of your judgement. I use to think Breathwork was the "cure-all" but "Time" has taught me it is the cure-all along with perseverance.

I concluded the day with another breathing circle in synchronicity with the Annual Day of Breath Awareness on January 22nd. I offered my Thirteen Breath technique to the group of five people and smiled as I kept a loving eye on them knowing they are only scratching the surface of what our breath has to offer us. It is when we choose to dedicate ourselves to a daily or regular practice that we will truly know the depth of Breathwork.

Breathing Circle

I use to offer weekly breathing circles back East in the early 2000s. I did it for a couple of years and quit. Then I started up again in 2013 after my second awakening. That is when I met Natalie who started breathingcircle.com. I represent the San Diego breathing circle that meets the last Tuesday of the month for donations. In a breathing circle there is not a specific style of Breathwork that is the preferred style. It is left up to the facilitator. If you go to their website you will find more information of course and a world map showing the Breathing circle locations and times.

I do a variety of breathing circles to keep it interesting for me. I like the emotional quality certain music can add to a breathwork session. I also like when I don't even hear the music being played; when it fades from my consciousness and time and space dissolve into a vibrant intergetic continuous form of infinite possibilities, yet to be brought into this 3D reality.

My Experience

Tonight I offered a breathing circle inspired by some Facebook comments of people dreading the inauguration of the forty-fifth President. I gave them an opportunity to breathe through this historic event. There were only four of us. So instead of facilitating, I joined them in breath because they were regulars, (no one new showed up). I played a nice piece of music titled 'Listen' by Jonathon Alexander or Alexander Jonathon. (If you ever meet him tell him to give me a call. I would like to thank him for his music.)

I played the Beatles song 'Come Together' to get us moving with dance. I asked my fellow breathers to spin 360 degrees at least once. Towards the end of the song I offered some standing Bhastrika or Transformational 100 breath technique or warriors breath if you are a Supreme Science Qi Gong follower. One would reach their hands up on the inhale and exhale pulling the arms down and knee up, repeat and switch legs. When the song ended we laid down to breathe and started with shaking our legs and thumping our arms on the floor with a sound of choice or an Om as Listen started to play.

We settled into our own breathing pattern with a couple of suggestions I offered to the group. Then I let them be like a good Holotropic practitioner and focused on my conscious connected breath. The overall session was surreal. My neck started hurting at one point and I went into plow pose to stretch it out while maintaining my breath and then into a full shoulder stand with my arms up by my side and hands at the hips thinking like any good yogi somebody should take a picture of this. To balance that pose I went into a full wheel or back bend with a nice stretch from my armpits to my genitalia to a dolphin pose, the whole time maintaining a nice rhythmic breath. Back down to my flat back or Savasana and everything for me shifted. I tuned into my fellow breathers intuitively and empathetically for a moment since I was the facilitator and then back in to the consciousness before me.

I went past the light and dark into the nothingness before I took form, before I had a thought, before I became sound, light, dark, color or motion. It was before "I" there is just "IS" and I was in absolute raw pure stillness, deep space. I am that. It was neutral yet powerful beyond measure. I was in total recognition of it in me. It was a place I have avoided in the past but tonight totally embraced. I surrendered. After that realization I got up to get my note pad to write a note down so I wouldn't forget because I knew I was definitely in an altered state of awareness.

I continued to breathe and raise my vibration. I empathetically and intuitively felt each person in the room and thought to get up and help them but let it go. I was breathing tonight. I had a vision of serving food or energy to a long line of people nourishing them, feeding them, helping them. I chanted OM on the inhale and exhale. I have not been able to do the exhale sound for some time now and there it was just like ten years ago when I toned and practiced just about every day. I had insights to a breath circle that if we were tuned in like babies, empathic and sounded off with others to join them in their suffering to help them completely express their pain leaving nothing but the innocence that was once so easily enjoyed.

My creative mind was very active with future ideas, visions and colors. I finally sat up in lotus position to meditate with my eyes half closed to witness deep shades of energetic purple energy shapeshifting about the room. I sat, vibrated and broadcast love, light and deep space out into the conscious world, into the ever-changing evolving world where the 1% have been revealed for what they are and it is all going to change and shift into a new paradigm with a balance of another 1%, us, the awakened ones.

Slowly everyone made their way to a seated position and we sat in silence for a little while. Then we shared and discussed our experience and how much more we have to learn and let go of. We recognized our connection to each other and validated this intuitive part of ourselves, agreeing we should express ourselves in the moment during our session and group energy. I was feeling fantastic and happy to have company and eager to write this part down while I was still vibrating in the loving energy that is always right here, just a couple breaths away.

After proofreading my writing from cover to cover again, I considered changing my writing on Om and what I believed a year ago because this breath session gave me a deeper understanding of the ancient Yogi's writings. Sound comes before the division of light and dark out of the nothingness or space. I use the words nothingness and space because I do not have a word or words for that forgotten essence. I am still digesting this experience as it is outside of what I thought I understood. Creating one more file in the synaptic gaps of my brain.

It is time for me to maintain my daily breath sessions and to meditate regularly to radiate and increase this frequency of being in my life.

Here are my suggestions: Find a Breathworker or:

1. Trust yourself, your gut, your intuitive self.
2. Find a safe space.
3. Set as aside three hours of your life.
4. Invite a trust worthy friend to join you.
5. Go on to Spotify and pull up a Holotropic mix lasting forty-five minutes to an hour.
6. Consciously Breathe.
7. When the music ends, draw, paint or write. Be creative.
8. Put it away. Look at it in a few days or a week.

How do you feel now?

We don't need more Buddhists in the world.

We need more Buddhas.

We don't need more Christians in the world.

We need more Christ-like people.

Dan Brule

Micro Cosmic Orbit

Traditional Chinese Medicine

The first Breathwork workshop I participated in back in 1992, I discovered an energy line circling the middle of my body from my head to my pelvic floor. It went down my back curving around in between my legs and back up my belly and chest. It was subtle but distinct for me. I also energetically found my perineum, a key area to relax during my Breathwork session. Relaxing the subtlest tension in that area made all the difference and changed the direction my life was headed. It is why I am writing another Breathing book twenty five-years later.

Back then I thought I discovered something new but in my search for understanding of what had happened to me during that life changing weekend workshop, I came across some books and one that described the Micro Cosmic Orbit (MCO). I found out the Traditional Chinese Medicine people have known about it for thousands of years. I thought, "So I am not the first one. But why haven't I heard about it?" Even to this date there are Breathworkers out there that still do not know about the MCO. This doesn't surprise me because of what I am still learning and discovering at conferences, like the Global Inspirational Conference (GIC) and Breathwork Immersions (BI). The GIC and BI have taught me there is still more to learn and experience, and to stay humble and grateful for the little I do know.

The MCO is my general "go to" breath. I take the slowest inhale detailing the MCO all the way around from the roof of my mouth back to the tip of my tongue on one inhale. Sometimes as slow as one minute to complete the inhale with a relaxed exhale, repeating it several times. I consider the MCO the complete breath because it includes expansion in my back.

The MCO is a circular breath consisting of two meridians (energy channels). Starting at the roof of the mouth, up around the inside of the skull, down the spine to the perineum (the middle of the pelvic floor) is the governing meridian. From the perineum up the front of the body to the tip of the tongue is the conceptional or functional meridian. Breathing this circular breath helps me/you breathe through every habitual and emotional breathing pattern established in our psyche. It is a wonderful way to purify my body, mind and heart and raise my vibration, frequency and harmonics.

I have included a graphic for a visual understanding and one of my healing experiences at the end of this book to further validate the power of Breathwork, Conscious Breathing, believing (faith) and why it is my general go to breath.

Micro Cosmic Orbit

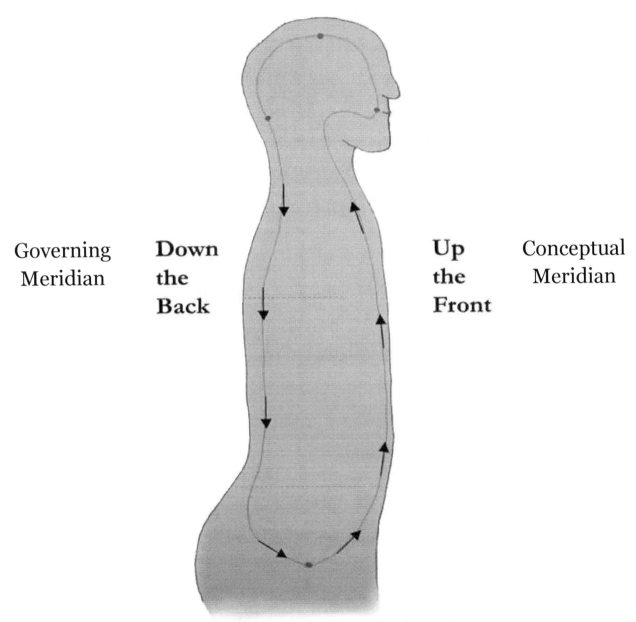

Governing Meridian   **Down the Back**   **Up the Front**   Conceptual Meridian

Around Through the Perineum

Thirteen Breaths to Freedom

Thirteen Breaths to Freedom started out as my personal maintenance and secret breathing practice. I could do it in my parked car, a stairwell, on the beach or the bushes near the BMX track, anywhere I could take a couple of minutes to breathe with intention without interruption. It is the way I have maintained my deep connection to spirit, insight and intuition. Back in the nineties I averaged about three of these mini-breath sessions a day and that is how the "Thirteen Breaths to Freedom" came to be.

Almost a decade after my awakening, I started teaching Thirteen Breath workshops without much success based in a little town named Fuquay Varina, NC. It was there that I realized very few people had heard of Breathwork during my talks and advertising trials, exploring different words to describe and entice consumers and soul searchers to give Breathwork a try. That is where my subtitle of my second book came from. If something is new it needs a proper introduction; hence, "An Introduction to Breathwork".

Finally during a round trip flight I heard this from two different people, "You should write a book" one on the outbound flight and one on the return. That made it the third time, a charm, my Toastmaster mentor Steve said, "You should write a book. It will give you more authority." the very nature in which I rebel. I wish he would have said recognition, respect or understanding but he said, "Authority." I shied away from that word until that return flight. It was then I looked up at the vast cloudy blue sky, as I have since I was kid, like there is a God up there somewhere dictating commands for my life. So I said, "Okay! I will write a book." and I did. I was not told anything about promoting it, so it sat for about two years. I was just happy to be finished with it like I am almost finished with this one. The difference being is this one has come with a promotional guide line, grassroots across the country movement. I get overwhelmed thinking about it, so I don't.

I am learning to let things unfold in their own way. Currently the seed of this book is germinating as I type this sentence. I wear all the hats at the moment; Cover design, interior design, editing with help from some wonderful friends, marketing and massaging my own shoulders at times after raking my fingers through my hair. And of course consciously breathing and feeling and wow! It finally feels complete. YAY! What a journey this has been. I hope you have enjoyed reading it and received something of value from it as much as I have writing it.

I have included a Thirteen Breath cheat sheet, more breathing info and a couple more of my healing stories. And for your information most of these Breathwork styles are trademarked and/or copyrighted. It is best to look into that before copying or retitling one as your own. I love finding the origin and the story of how they came to be.

Now you know I am not officially trained or certified in any of the fore mentioned styles of Breathwork. I am self-trained and continued practicing what I learned in a book or workshop long after I read or experienced it. I am still learning to trust my subtle quiet inner voice, that inner part of myself and my spirit's guidance. I am certified to teach yoga with only two percent of this training devoted to pranayama. At this time there is not a licensing board for Breathworkers in the United States but I am sure there will be, one day soon.

Not all of us will have the opportunity or be able to afford workshops, trainings, programs or travel to specific Breathwork gatherings. But we all have the time to Breathe.

There is no absolute right way to breathe but there are more productive ways and I hope this workbook helps you find one that works for you.

Explore

Trust

Intend

Thirteen Breaths to Freedom©

Micro cosmic orbit aka circular breathing: Inhale around the inside of your skull, down your back, around through the perineum, up the front, belly, heart and upper chest. Surrender/relax/ let go on the exhale with a little squeeze at the end before inhaling.

I love my body
I love my mind   } Detailed slow breath
I love my heart

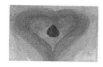

Relax the jaw breathe in and out through your mouth, big belly, relaxed exhale only. No squeeze.

My body is relaxed
My mind is at peace   } Exhale = relaxed "ha"
My heart is open

I am alive
I am focused   } Breathe in through pursed lips,
I am connected   Exhale = relaxed "ha"

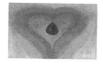

I love myself   } Breathe in through pursed lips
I love my life   Exhale = HEAVY "ha"
I am love   fill lungs quickly to capacity; quick inhale

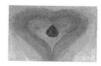

I AM   } Hold breath after inhale
                          Just let go on exhale, be the witness
                          Let your body resume natural breathing

89

Thirteen Breaths to Freedom Notes

How were the affirmations for you?

How was the sequence?

Did you understand when to hold your breath? And why?

Was there a revelation?

Did you feel a connection or energy?

What would you ask a client or student?

Notes:

More Breathing Information

Hyperventilation refers to over-breathing, in which ventilation exceeds the metabolic demand and its related physiological consequences. In other words, breathing out more than you are breathing in, to keep it simple.

Tetany (or Tetney) refers to an imbalance within the body between your alkaline and acidic state, which in turn may cause cramps in various parts of your body. This is my simplistic view of this phenomenon on a physical level. On a mental emotional level some refer it to as control issues. I might ask you to look for some unexpressed anger or something that has not been forgiven that gives your ego drive and purpose.

Vegetotherapy is a form of Reichian psychotherapy that I came across in my research It involves physical manifestations and it is used as a way to disarm our body amour, from the way we hold ourselves, from posture to the way we dress our bodies. It is worth looking into.

Websites:

ibfgic.com

IBF   ibfnetwork.com

GPBA   breathworkalliance.com

doasone.com

Breathing Circle.com

rebirthingbreathwork.com

catherinedowling.com

breathmastery.com

transformationalbreath.com

thepresenceprocessportal.com

sondraray.com

claritybreathwork.com

holotropic.com

holographic-breathing.com

breathingcenter.com

icemanwimhof.com

coherentbreathing.org

mentalphysics.net

breatheology.com

And many others....

Trust the Breath, trust your body and trust your heart, the intelligence within and around it. Have you ever questioned a yawn, a sneeze or a cough? Trust the process. Question the mind.

Notes

Meditation

On February 8, 2017, I woke up with a belly full of yesterday's dinner and late night snacks wondering when I am going to stop doing this to myself. I could feel the lump of carrot cake with cream cheese frosting, so tasty, just sitting in my gut. I thought I need to discipline me more and the next thought was, today has now become a day of silence, a day devoted to meditation and simple plant-based food, spring water and this piece of writing.

I went to the bathroom, washed my face, drank some water, turned off my phone, grabbed my meditation cushion, cleared out the bottom of my closet and sat down closing the door in front of me. The time was 7:11. My goal was to sit in stillness for an hour. I pushed open the door and rolled out of my lotus position at 8:23 much to my surprise.

I was filled with gratitude, a big thank you to life, all of it and that includes you. My mind wandered all over my current concerns and a few past and distant with time. I thought about how long I have known about meditation and how little I use this wonderful exercise. I was hoping to write some beautiful experience to share with you but I simply witnessed my undisciplined mind jump from thought to memory as I would try to keep it focused on my third eye.

In the moments of absolute concentration I noticed my left eye was more dominant than my right, while searching for that perfect balance between both eyes. I was looking for the proper spot in between my brows that reveals the light of God. "Make thy eyes one" is a teaching from many different schools of meditation. My current influence is Yogananda's school of Self-Realization, a fellowship for devotees. One of his teachers told him you have mastered the technique but do not forget about the purpose.

I remembered a lady I met years ago when I first started teaching meditation that told me she had been meditating for twenty years and nothing has ever happened in her meditation. She described how she would silence her mind and that was it. I asked her, "What is your intention?

"To be still, relaxed, silent and peaceful" she responded.

"Then you have succeeded," I said, "Change your intention if you want more."

Catching that memory I focused back on my spine moving the subtle energy up to the back of my head and across to my third eye doing my best to focus both of my mortal eyes there with a feeling of love and gratitude for my creator.

When I felt my knees and feet start to go numb and my spine slightly slump I would flex them, contracting various muscles including my glutes, to get my blood and energy flowing again. These were the signs that my hour was about up.

There are many schools of meditation and they are all worth checking out before settling down to one. Yogananda sought out many teachers before finding his Guru and devoting himself to that linage. I highly recommend his autobiography audio book and the teachings you can receive through snail mail.

Here in the West meditation has become another word for stress reduction and relaxation exercises forgetting its original purpose: Self-Realization or connection to God. Someone is usually talking the whole time, guiding you or reminding you to stay focused. And there is most likely some new age music playing in the background. I consider this more a form of entertainment. It doesn't sound as good if you called it visualization exercises. Is this because we have a hard time doing nothing?

I know nothing. I teach nothingness and I want to take you to a place with no name.

After writing the rough draft of this piece I went for a jog and yoga in the local park. I jogged breathing through my nose through the freshly rain rinsed canyons. I heard hawks cry out and lizards scamper through the underbrush as I jogged by. My mind was clear and I received another idea and more words for my book cover, 'A journey with breath' and clarity of the meaning behind the phrase. Simply put, 'Breath = God'. This invisible field between us and the clouds and ozone is what sustains and protects this way of life. It is connected and shared by everything and everyone on this planet.

During my silent yoga on the vibrant healthy green grass that felt so full of life and happy, I had a deeper realization in my first forward fold that continued with everything is connected. My hamstrings were demanding my attention and when I backed off of them and relaxed the back of my neck I was able to feel more of my whole body. I noticed more of my weight was on my heels and not balanced across the bottom of my foot. With that sensation I followed the feeling up the back of my legs around my buttocks down my back and neck and on out to my fingertips. Every-stretched-body part had an equal awareness to it and from that energetic sensation and consciousness as I went through my variation of sun salutation that ended with a handstand. I was very aware of my connected state of being in that moment.

As I reworked the cover of this book with my new insights on my computer I caught myself thinking out loud a couple of times, telling my computer "I know I can do this, help me out."

If a man thinks out loud and no one is around is he still in silence?

For my midday meditation I decided to go to Yogananda's Garden in Encinitas, CA. It was a perfect day to ride through the mystical coastline fog to keep my mind in a connected joyful state. I went to my usual spot on the circular bench facing an ornate tree. I sat on my gloves because I know it doesn't take long for my sits bones to get tired of the concrete bench. Once I had adjusted myself into my meditation posture I closed my eyes and immediately felt a presence around me and in front of me. I thought and felt, "Wow!" as a figure started to appear before my gently closed eyes. It was like I was 'star struck' and in awe of such a presence. The feeling was; they were pleased with my work so far and then my excited and surprised mind started to garble up the frequency like a car stereo driving out of reach of the radio station's broadcast. It felt wonderful. I was right, the discipline is necessary or I will miss out on more of these beautiful moments. It's time to tune up and tune in again.

I concluded the day with one final sitting meditation in my closet that only lasted twenty minutes. I finished in my bed under the covers with detailed relaxation and MCO breathing before sleep came while focusing on my third eye. As I looked for the light I realized I am in my way, or better put; my ego is in the way, my identity and knowing of James. The question I posed was, how do I get around that part of myself?

My answer:

Daily practice.

I might not meditate in the traditional sense as much as I used to but I do consciously breathe at different times throughout the day and it feels very good. I know I could always do more but why when there are so many good movies to watch, like Inside Out, Dr. Strange and The Shed.

Here is a short list of meditations and places I have checked out in the past:

- **Edgar Cayce Search for God** series and classes
- **Buddhism** there are many. Here is one is of the chants: Nam-myoho-renge-kyo (nom yo hu rong gay kyo)
- **A Course in Miracles** I have yet to finish this course. I have started many times.
- **Vipassana** reintroduced in 1969 by Mr. S.N. Goenka. It is a ten-day silent residential program.
  I liked this honest man's statement before we started our silence: "I just smoked my last cigarette and I am about to spend to 10 days in silence with the person I hate the most, me." I was impressed. He ended up sitting behind me and I missed his presence the hours he missed our meditation but I understood.
- Moving meditations: Qi Gong, Tai Chi and Hatha and Yin Yoga

Meditation is about our inner experience, stilling the body and its senses, focusing the mind, opening the heart, remembering and recalling, the divine spark of life that you are. I am. You will know when you made it by the state of gratitude you feel and express.

Breathwork is the quickest way I know to get into deep meditation. It is the cleansing storm before the calm, clear mind.

Recommendations:

- Create a place or alter
- Set a time (two minutes to start)
- Daily Practice

Note how the energy of your space and how it changes over time. How your body responds to your alter.

Grounded Tooth Fairy

"I don't want to drive ground rods for the fire alarm panels." I told Greg in an overwhelmed tone. "I have enough work to last me the rest of the year."

"Come on James, I've taken good care of you. Just help me out with these ground rods." I sighed, "All right it's the last thing I will do on this job." And it was.

I went around town looking for a fence post driver and couldn't find one. So I grabbed my eight pound sledgehammer and headed out to the job with my helper. Standing on a six foot ladder in the grass pounding ten foot long five eighths thick copper cladded ground rods into the orange clay soil of North Carolina was not my idea of a good time. I called Greg and told him I needed a fence post driver and that I was not going to finish the ground rods until I got one. He asked the guys in the fire alarm sprinkler division to make me one.

We called it the iron cross. It was made out of two-inch sprinkler pipe with a tee in the middle. The top end had a pot metal steel cap tack welded in place for extra strength. The two handles on each side stuck out about six inches designed to hold on to it while sliding the two foot two inch piece up and down pounding the ground rod into the earth.

Back at the job I gave the iron cross to my young helper who tried tapping the ground rod into the ground. I said, "Pound it like a man. Put some muscle into it." He looked at me and continued tapping the ground rod. Then I said, "Get out of the way. Let me show you how to do it." I grabbed that iron cross and slammed the ground rod and watch it move six inches into the earth. I slammed it a couple more times sinking the ground rod several inches at a time, showing my helper how a man does it. Then I slammed it one last time. The next thing I knew I was laying crumpled up on the ground with stars flitting around my head dazed and confused. Better me than my helper who was in complete shock.

The ground rod popped through the end of the iron cross. The force I created and the grip I had on the cross being guided by a firmly planted ground rod pulled the two of us together right at the height of my face. I collided with the iron cross, as my arms drug it down my nose, lips and the front of my body that fell forward. The traumatized look on my helper's face told me more than I wanted to know. I tore up my face, cracked my nose and my right front incisor tooth pointed backwards into my mouth. I was pissed. I knew I didn't want to drive these damn ground rods into the ground. The power of the dollar got me again.

I told my helper to gather up the tools and meet me at my work van. "You're driving me to my dentist" I said before I went to sit in my van. Once I settled in the passenger seat I relaxed my body and mind, calming myself into a positive state of being for the healing to begin by breathing the MCO. It felt weird having my tooth pointing backward into my mouth. It was so foreign to me and surreal like any so called accident, one moment all is normal and the next all is being questioned.

I played with my tooth with my tongue as I continued to relax on my way to the dentist by slowly breathing the Micro Cosmic Orbit breaths that can induce a euphoric state. In my relaxed and intuitive state I felt I could pop my tooth back in place. I put my thumb on it to try, but it felt firmly planted behind my other teeth.

When we arrived at the dentist's office I was taken in pretty quick after they saw my face, my tooth and heard my story. Sitting in the dentist's chair, I was told what they were going to do. The dentist said she would give me a shot of Novocain and then pop my tooth back in place. I said, "Like this," and reached in my mouth with my thumb and popped the tooth back in place with extra force this time. Both the assistant and the dentist cringed when it popped back in place with a snap. Then I said, "I thought I could do that but I just wasn't sure it was the best thing to do."

"Your tooth is dead and you will need a root canal." The dentist said after she composed herself and continued, "First it will turn brown, then black and we will pull it out fill it with some pink goop and put it back in with a bridge behind it. No one will be able to tell the difference."

"No, I will heal my tooth and that won't be necessary." I said looking at her puzzled face.

"You don't seem to understand, your tooth is dead the nerve ending has been severed." looking at me in wonder.

"No you don't seem to understand," I calmly but defiantly replied. We went back and forth a couple of times before I looked right into her determined eyes and said, "You don't know who I am. I will heal this tooth," and I got up and left.

I told my wife and kids the whole story, about smashing my face and the disagreement with the dentist after popping the tooth back in myself. My kids laughed at me with random comments. Like, "Right dad! Sure you can. You're funny. You think you are going to heal yourself. " and giggled some more. My wife just looked at me with a feeling of, 'I wish you would just keep your mouth shut.' She was always wishing that or so it felt to me.

That night as I was going to sleep I continued doing my healing work in bed. I said my intentions to my higher self and asked for assistance with my healing for the highest good. I woke up in the morning and my tooth was turning brown. My kids had another good laugh while I remained quiet. I went by the dentist's office on my way to the job to schedule an appointment for the root canal. They politely smiled at me as they proudly flipped through the pages of their schedule book and told me they couldn't get me in for thirty days. I said, "Then I have thirty days to heal myself," and turned to walk out before another word was said. I felt they wanted me to be embarrassed with a black tooth for a while.

I told Greg everything that had happened including the part about healing myself and then showed him my brown tooth. He said nothing but shook his head in a doubtful way.

I became quiet about my tooth with the people in my life. No one seemed to understand where I was coming from. During the day I would press up on my tooth with my thumb driving down the road imagining the nerve reconnecting to it. During the night I would say my intentions, ask my highest self for help with the healing and slowly breathe the Micro Cosmic Orbit with great detail. I would breathe with the concentrated awareness of the life force energy, moving it down my back and around and up the front of my body as I breathed in. I did this several nights in a row without doubt and a determined desire to walk my talk and live my words.

Then one night when I was breathing that loving energy down my spine, around my pelvic floor and up the front of my body and it changed directions on its own. I relaxed my control and surrendered to be a witness of the energy moving without my conscious will or mental direction. It changed directions just below my heart and went back down my belly, around my groin in between my legs and up the back of my body. It went up the back of my neck, around the inside of my skull and down into my brown tooth with a little tick or click of a sound. The sensation was wonderful to say the least and I smiled knowing I was healed. I rolled over and fell into a deep grateful sleep.

The next morning I woke up and went right to our bathroom mirror to look at my white tooth. It was healed. Then I proceeded to show my children and my wife. My kids were quiet when I pointed at my white tooth and said, "Daddy healed himself. See, it's white." They just looked confused and didn't ask questions or comment just sat there drop jawed. My wife on the other hand had an expression on her face that was a cross between "I don't believe it" and "Oh God, now he will never keep his mouth shut now."

After breakfast I went by the dentist's office to cancel my root canal appointment much to their surprised silence and bewilderment. I told Greg and smiled at his expression of disbelief. Then I went off to do another job that he threw my way. I was feeling quietly proud of myself and my beliefs, and very grateful knowing I was walking my talk and being an example of what is possible for us humans if we really choose to believe and apply ourselves.

I now know we can heal our bodies, minds and hearts. If I can do it, you certainly can do it.

A new question has popped into my mind. How big is this onion? How many more layers are there for me to unravel? I am constantly and pleasantly being surprised and humbled by Breathwork and meditation and the revelations I experience. More of my life's experiences will shared in a "Post Pranayama and Breathwork 6X9 book. A journey with breath making peace."

God Issues

I was attending a kinesiology workshop in 1993 that was focusing on mom and dad issues. We were doing kinesiology (muscle testing) in pairs. My understanding of kinesiology is, you use your muscles to help get around your mind and into your subconscious. You then have a better understanding of yourself, and why you are the way you are. You are asked to hold your arm out straight in front of your body, parallel to the floor making a fist. Then your partner asks a yes or no question and pushes down on your arm. If your arm remains strong that is a yes. If your arm becomes weak that is a no and you have something to work on.

I told my partner, "I am finished with mom and dad. I have issues with God and I want to work on my God issues not my parents." She confirmed what I said by testing my arm strength. Then I told her I wanted to go straight to the source where it all began. Then the facilitator Cindy came over to check on our progress.

My partner responded, "James is good with mom and dad and he is working on God."

Cindy replied in a loud tone broadcasting across the room, "Nobody is done with mom and dad, let me check him." I raised my arm for her to ask the testing questions. She asked my partner to place her hand on the back of mine. Then she covered my partner's hand with hers. She asked if I was OK with mom, my arm remained strong, meaning I was OK. Then she asked if I was OK with dad and I felt her push harder the second time and then she said, "See, he's still needs to work on dad."

The facilitator asked my partner if she felt the difference and my partner replied, "Yes, it felt like you pushed harder the second time." I was elated to have a bold partner stand by me again; elementary school was a long time ago. Cindy on the other hand was not and walked off in a huff.

We broke for lunch and I chose not to eat with the group and found an empty parking lot to be alone and continue with my God issues. I practiced my modified breathwork technique that I learned at the Ecstasy Breathing Workshop to help me better understand this core issue. My intention was to get to the root of the problem, with hope that it wouldn't sprout up again. My working on mom and dad as much as I did, cleared the way so I could take hold of the trunk and follow it to the roots. So there I was breathing into my God issue with sincere emotion and intention sitting behind the steering wheel of my work truck off in a corner of a fairly empty parking lot. The Breathwork left me with a clear mind and a major part of my ego dissolved. I breathed progressively faster up to the point I hold my breath and then I had this memory or vision as I relaxed into the exhale.

I was a glowing sphere of light that became conscious of its self. I allowed little separate conscious specks of light to become independent from me, their source, the big glowing sphere of light. First I would do little jumps like bouncing on and off the bigger piece of myself. I became immersed and focused within the little speck of light like I am now with this Earth experience being James. As I became more comfortable separating from the larger self, I would jump a little further each time. Upon returning I would be absorbed back into the light. I learned I could float out and away, further and further into the dark potent empty space around the light. I would turn to look back at the large sphere of light and a feeling of love would ignite from within me, my consciousness and I would dash back to be completely absorbed into the oneness like a really good nap of sleep. The awareness of "I" would completely disappear.

With each jump or flight, I grew more confident with this state of awareness and stayed away a little longer each time. I was always aware of the bigger piece of myself, until one flight took me further into the void and the potential unknown than I ever went.

I stopped to float in the nothingness and turned to look back at the large light, home, and it was nowhere to be found. The familiar loving glow from within was replaced by a jolt of shock, disbelief, anxiety and "Panic!" I began to flit across the emptiness in all directions, searching for the light at the pace of a panting breath, back and forth, up and down, diagonal, zig zags, forgetting the realization, I am the light.

Ah Ha! My slumped body of consciousness thought sitting in the front of my work truck. I had discovered one of the major roots, underlying many of my problems. Abandonment! I thought God abandoned me. I had blamed God for leaving me, when it was I that left God and forgot I am that.

I felt absolutely incredible with this discovery that I returned to the workshop and told my aunt Julianna, the assistant workshop facilitator, "I am done. I am going home. I am good." She looked me in the eye and recognized I spoke the truth, and then asked if I would stay until the end, in a feel-sorry-for-Cindy kind of way. I agreed and spent the second half of the workshop with the only other man there. We were put in a private room, all by ourselves, as outcasts from the rest of the group, women. I guess he didn't play along either.

I was glad I stayed because I met Jill who received information through sacred geometry that I found intriguing. It became another fun tool for my path of self-discovery and realization at that time. I kept my God experience and Breathwork practice very close to my heart, not sharing it for a very long time.

Later in my Body Mind and Spirit Expo days I met a lady going by the name Sage. She told me we all have three main core issues to understand and process about ourselves. She believed most everything we go through can be boiled down to these 3 issues:

1. Fear   The unknown
2. Abandonment   Separation
3. Self-worth or self-esteem   Love of self

I find a lot of truth in her words and added the right hand column for further understanding.

I heard Carolynn Myss tell a story about being allowed to come up and take three breaths of the freshest cleanest blue sky air and then be thrown back down into the grey smoky soot. After that you will try for the rest of your life to get back up to the clean fresh air.

It was around this time I felt so good and satisfied I thought I could die and I would be perfectly fine. It was like I had taken three of the wonderfully described breaths and then I was thrown back down with the message "Do it again. Find your way back up here on your own."

Reviewing, writing and integrating my own past stories I see the difference between then and now. Then I had a beautiful wife that made me look good and three adorable well behaved children that made me proud. I had a secure job that provided for the house, car in the driveway and food on the table plus some fun. I had a good social life. I felt very content and satisfied with myself and attainments at that time, I had reached a pinnacle.

But when all of that was taken away I was lost. I was basing a good percentage of my contentment on the outside world. One of the thoughts I constantly thought around that time was:

"I want to die but retain all my knowledge."

What I meant was, "When I die I want to retain all of the knowledge I have so my next life will be easier." The other thing I noticed about my life was I couldn't see my life past the age of fifty; it was a void, an unknown.

I wasn't planning on living this long and a lot of my old friends are surprised I am still around. The subtle truth I am starting to recognize is, the old me is dying or dead, and I have not acknowledged that yet. It is an earth-bound ghost of me not completely released but dead.

This all falls under: "Be careful what you ask for!" I am starting over at 55. The universe is listening. It is responding to our minds, from simple thoughts, to fantastic thoughts; from intentions prayers and emotional energetic broadcasts to the continuous silent repetitive subtle unnoticed everyday thoughts. I know this, I apply this, I have experienced this and I forget it all at the same time. I am amazed at what I have created for myself and I am constantly accepting the life before me like I had no input into its creation, and no responsibility for its outcomes. Sitting here writing this I can easily pontificate this reality and then I go hop in my car and slip in to a prewritten program of predictable responses to drivers that don't think or drive like I do. "Gas pedal is on the right" is one of my favorite sayings before I catch myself not living in the moment and back off and breathe creating peace and ease. What's my hurry with this human race?

Clarity Breathwork asks some really good questions too. One of them is similar to this:

What is it you really want?

I have a question too;

Are you ready to breathe?

In peace,

With love,

James

My handbook for life.

PS

There's more. I feel another book starting brew, beyond the follow up of this writing.

Here's a clue.

The Cover

The cover has twelve overlapping layered hearts, half exposed and half hidden, circling the thirteenth. Ideally the center heart would be behind, set back, within and underneath the layers of hearts representing the archetypes of being human. The master is only realized from within once he or she has recognized the layers of the human self. A master understands all the conscious and subconscious layers of the self, the light and dark of each archetype that has been or is currently being played out as a conscious role within him or her.

The balanced, aware, secure and complete heart reveals both the light and dark halves in the middle as equals, representing the master within. Within this complete heart, the center of our being, there is a source, a divine spark, an eternal flame giving life to everything. It is the connecting force with the permeating energetic spiral traveling through space and time weaving together the layers of archetypes.

There is no hero without a victim, no healer without the sick, no lover without a hater, no creation without destruction, no ruler without the subservient, no innocent without the guilty, no regular people without the strange, no warrior without a pacifist, no seeker without a quitter, no knower or without the stuck, no outlaw without the police, no jester without the serious, no sage without the ignorant and no magician without the incompetent.

The unconditional love from the center heart has compassion and patience for us all.

Let us find our center.

The master disciplines the self.

The master knows thy self.

Made in the USA
San Bernardino, CA
29 May 2017